Go Disciple:

BE ONE, MAKE ONE

Chad W. Hood

Go Disciple
Be One, Make One

Published by Rainer Publishing
www.rainerpublishing.com

ISBN 978-0692319345

Typeset in 10pt Heuristica by Ashton Designs
www.ashtondesigns.co.uk

Printed in the United States of America

Acknowledgements

Dedicated to the ones who have poured into my life as a young man.

My Dad, Don, who shared the gospel with me. Dad, thanks for letting me interrupt you when I came forward in the middle of your sermon. Jonathan and I are both pastors and that says something. I love you both.

The staff at First Baptist Woodstock: Pastor Johnny Hunt, Tony Nolan, and John Franklin who helped me to understand and experience the nearness of God. So many good things have come from my time there like my friendship with Jason Davidson who has put up with me for the past 16 years and walked with me through the ups and downs of life. JD, a man could not have asked for a better friend.

Finally, to Heather, my beautiful bride, I would definitely not be the man I am today and most likely would not have made it if it had not been for you. God knew what I needed. Thank you for walking with me and for your tireless work with our family and ministry.

Special thanks to my family at Bay Leaf.

It is an honor to serve with you and the staff.

Thank you Pastor Ron and Pastor Marty for the opportunity to serve alongside of you.

Contents

Introduction

L ET ME EXPLAIN THE REASON YOU ARE HOLDING this book. At a specific moment in time, God gave me a burden. Here is how it happened.

It was one of those moments, an instance where something is birthed in your heart and alters the way you see everything. At that moment you have to decide whether you will proceed down a specific path or miss the opportunity in front of you.

My moment occurred a few years ago. I was in a closed country where people are not free to talk about Jesus with others. I was sitting in a second floor room with a missionary leader from that area in Central Asia, and he was talking about the team in that particular city and the fact that they needed more men for the work there. He explained that in these Central Asian and Middle Eastern cultures, it was practically impossible to evangelize across gender lines. Men were needed to reach men.

I listened for a while and finally had to ask the question, "Why aren't they getting more men on the field?" His answer astonished me and then convicted me at the same time. He said that around 50 percent of the young men who applied to the mission board were deferred and around 30 percent of the young women. "Why?" I asked. He responded by telling me that it was a whole host of reasons, from particular sins such as pornography within a year, to family issues, and everything in between. Most are deferred and told they can reapply in a year. Some were permanently turned down for service.

I left that meeting shocked and disturbed. I began to pray about the situation and to seek the Lord about the whole matter. In the next two days God did an amazing work in my life. I was consumed with this problem. How could God change these statistics and how could He use me? These young men and women were not your average college students out looking for a good time. They were willing to go to hard places for the sake of the gospel, and they were being turned down. This problem was absolutely unacceptable, and I was not looking the other way. Over the next 24 hours as I traveled back to the U.S., God gave me a vision for what was needed, how it needed to be done, and how it had to begin with Him doing a work in my heart.

As soon as I landed in the States I called a good friend who was the dean at a local Christian college. I asked if there was any time we could meet over the next few days. He was completely booked for the next two weeks. He said that he would let me know if anything opened up.

The next morning, I went into talk with Marty Jacumin, my senior pastor at the church where I serve as associate pastor. I told him what God had laid on my heart, and he affirmed what God was doing. In the middle of the conversation, my phone rang and it was the dean of the college. He said, "I had a cancellation and can do lunch today." I asked my pastor, and he said he was free as well. The three of us met an hour later.

The dean had been a missionary and was still extremely involved in the lives of young men and women. He was well aware of the issues facing this generation of would-be missionaries. At that lunch meeting I laid it all out and told him what I believed God was doing.

I gave him everything I had up to that point. The

program would be a one-semester, intense discipleship program. We would meet early in the morning—6 a.m.—for 13 weeks. This program would deal with the basic outline of deny yourself, take up your cross, and follow Jesus. These three critical points would be broken down in greater detail and expounded upon over the semester.

Additionally, we would break up the large group by gender once a week, with my wife meeting the girls. Along with these meeting times there would be a requirement of reading three specific books. I had also developed a schedule for morning and evening devotionals. I would work from the basic assumption that they knew nothing about walking with the Lord. My goal was simple: Encourage these young people to continue to pursue a relationship with God.

The radical aspect (which is not really radical at all) was a fast from television and Internet for two months. The only exception was checking email. What is a couple of months with no television or Internet when it comes to seeking God? This one aspect has proven to be critical in helping to understand simple self-denial in the process of seeking God.

The purpose of the class is to help students yield to God's work in their life, that they might in turn go make disciples. If they could get three months of intensive encouragement and accountability, their eyes might be opened to the glory of God. Hopefully, the trajectory of their life would be changed forever. They would go on to make disciples themselves, leading them quickly down a path of healing and spiritual health so that within a year's time the mission board process could begin again and lead to more missionaries on the field.

The dean loved the idea and confessed that it was

needed. He then told me that there was a man from the mission board on campus that day, and that I needed to talk with him as well. He gave me his name and number. Within 48 hours of me being back in the States, I had three crucial meetings and confirmation from God that I was headed in the right direction.

The third meeting was with a man from the mission board who was in charge of interviewing and evaluating the missionary applicants. My conversation with him helped me understand the process and what was actually happening. He told me in more detail why so many were turned away.

I started our conversation by asking, "What happens to these young men and women after deferral from the board?"

The answer was understandable but difficult. Those deferred were given the name of a counselor or church in their area that could be contacted for help. That was it.

He said, "Chad, we are simply not equipped to counsel after the fact, nor are we tasked with doing so."

I told him what God had put on my heart in Central Asia, and he was excited. His burden had always been for those who had been turned down. Specifically, his fear was that they would not seek help and never come back through the process. How tragic it is to think of a young man or woman losing their opportunity to go and fulfill what they believed to be God's call. He gave me insight and encouragement over the next two years as I continued to disciple and develop this program.

My conviction began with those turned away by missionary boards, but it soon grew to include more. My initial thoughts were for a *reactive* type of ministry. While that was an important part of the ministry, it was not the only part. The mission board was uncovering sin issues that had already existed. What about those who had not been through the mission board process? If 50 percent of those who had gone to the mission board had been rejected because of sin, what about all those other students and young adults? God expanded my thinking to involve a *proactive* as well as *reactive* idea of ministry.

So I piloted the program with some of my students. That next semester I took a group of young men through the beginning stages and concepts of what would become *Go Disciple*. God used that time in the life of those young men and women and encouraged me in a wonderful way.

As I dove in headfirst, I quickly understood I needed help and began to pray for it with no clue who that might be or how the help would come. Within in a few days of praying, a friend from the mission board contacted me about a young lady who was coming off of the field and wanted to work in discipleship as she finished up her term. She would be traveling on the weekends to conferences for the mission board for a year but during the week was to work at a local church. I was interested to say the least. All we would have to provide was a place to live and pay for regular work expenses. What I didn't know was that this missionary was a lady that I had worked with in Central Asia when God had laid all this on my heart. I received a call from the mission board and then a call from the missionary herself. I was amazed! We talked and agreed that God was moving in this and then we prayed for her a place to live.

The next day my wife informed me that a good friend of ours was looking for a young lady to live with her. It all worked out and now I had the help to get it done! There was no doubt that God was moving, and all I could do was follow behind Him in amazement. Within a few semesters there had been well over 100 people go through *Go Disciple*. God did some amazing things through those semesters and has taken those who have gone through the program all over the world.

Think about the multiplying power of discipleship. If these 100 students invested in 1 person each to disciple per year, teaching their mentees to disciple as well, then after 5 years the program would produce 3,200 sold out disciples. That is how we change the world with the gospel!

My burden began with young people. But the heart of this whole idea is that men and women, regardless of age, would be engaged in discipleship, grow, and then go and make disciples. This teaching is not geared to a specific age group and is meant for anyone who desires to grow and follow the Lord Jesus. It can be done on an individual basis, but it is intended to be read in the context of a discipleship relationship. Discussion is crucial for working out these concepts in the Christian life. I would encourage you to go through this book with a friend or mentor. After you go through it, you might even want to walk with someone else on his or her journey with Jesus.

This book follows the 13 weeks I developed for my course. Each chapter represents one week. I have condensed the 13-week program for book form, so you may go through these chapters at your pace, more quickly or more slowly. The big concepts covered in this book are just like the course I developed. First, deny yourself. Second, take up your cross. And third, follow Jesus. The point of the program is to be a jump-start or boost in your Christian walk. It has been referred to as a boot camp of sorts, but I prefer intensive discipleship. The intention is that within the 13-week period there is a radical redirection in your spiritual life and a new challenge to grow in your walk with Christ.

This book does not contain all the answers to your spiritual problems, it is merely a step in the process of learning to walk with Christ. Some who finish are not ready to disciple others, nor are they ready for the mission field. But all who walk through *Go Disciple* with a hunger and willingness to let God take them on a journey will go another step in their spiritual walk. I pray this book is a bold step for you in the right direction.

CHAPTER 1

The Message of the Church

THE MESSAGE OF THE CHURCH IS AND ALWAYS will be the gospel. The heart of that message is one of absolute and complete love as shown by the Father loving the world in such a way that He gave His only Son. With that offer of love, humanity has been invited to believe on the Lord Jesus Christ and to receive the salvation that He secured. Jesus took the penalty for our sin upon Himself at the cross. And not only did He pay the penalty for sin, but Jesus also secured life through the resurrection. In salvation, our sin is defeated and life is given. Through Christ, we are transferred from darkness and into light, from death into life.

With salvation comes the right to become children of God. Before salvation we were enemies of God, but now we have been reconciled to God through Christ Jesus our Lord. But even though this is a reality at the moment of salvation, we have to grow in our understanding of what this salvation means and what it looks like in life.

For example, let's consider a child is born into an aristocratic family. At birth the child does not understand the life in to which he has been born. He responds to physical desires such as his own hunger and comfort. As the child grows he learns to eat solid food, to use utensils, and speak words just like any other child. As that child becomes self-aware, his knowledge grows as to the expectations of his family. His actions begin to say something about who he is and the family to which he belongs. Hopefully, the child becomes an adult who is aware of the responsibility to his family, as well as his family's responsibility to others.

It is the same for the child of God. When we are born into the kingdom of God, it is only the beginning. From that point of inward change and rebirth we move on to growth in our understanding of God's truth. The Apostle Paul writes, "When I was a child, I spoke as a child, I understood as a child, I thought as a child; but when I became a man, I put away childish things."[1]

The follower of Jesus Christ is to mature, deepen, and to grow in wisdom and in understanding. The message of the church is one of salvation that leads to life and life is eternal. Where death speaks to decline and termination, life speaks of growth and maturing. If we have been given eternal life, then growth will be the natural progression of that life. Thus, the Christian is to grow into full maturity and that resembles the likeness of Jesus Christ.

This growth happens in the context of fellowship. The Apostle John writes, "That which we have seen and heard we declare to you, that you also may have fellowship with us; and truly our fellowship is with the Father and with His Son Jesus Christ. And these things we write to you that your joy may be full."[2]

The people of God have been brought into fellowship with the Father through the Lord Jesus Christ. Since each believer has been brought into that fellowship, each one shares in fellowship with the other. Therefore, the fellowship of the Spirit gives Christians the ability to be like-minded and to have the same love.[3] This unity leads believers to follow the Lord together.

The Apostle Paul refers to these followers as the "body of Christ" a number of times. The Head of the body is the Lord Jesus, and as the head controls the mortal body, so the Head controls the spiritual body. The head gives direction and purpose to the body. Jesus has given His body direction, power, and ability.

The heart of the body—the church—is one of love. Jesus, as the Head of the church, directs and empowers the body to love. The greatest command, Jesus would remark, was to love the Lord your God with all your heart, with all your soul, with all your strength, with all your mind, and to love your neighbor as yourself.[4]

Therefore, the church is to love God supremely and to love others in the same manner. The beauty of this truth is that the Spirit of God, given at the moment of salvation, seals the believer, gives life, and encourages growth in this love. [5] The believer is now part of the body and a partaker of the love of God. His love changes everything about the believer's life.

Now the believer is part of the body whose heart is one of love and devotion to God and to one another. Each part of the body is looking out not for his or her own interest but the interest of others. Those in the church looking out for each other should view the new believer as a spiritual child. As with any child, teaching and shepherding must occur for the child to grow into maturity. God has brought the believer into a community (the body) where that growth is to occur. The new believer not only hears and learns but also "sees" and learns what it means to follow Jesus Christ.

At the moment of His ascension, Jesus reminds his followers: "All authority in heaven and on earth has been given to me. Go therefore and make disciples of all nations, baptizing them in the name of the Father and of the Son and of the Holy Spirit, teaching them to observe all that I have commanded you." This passage in Matthew is called "The Great Commission."

Baptizing them in the name of the Father and the Son and of the Holy Spirit speaks to the beauty of salvation. We are saved and stand before the Father through the work of the Lord Jesus and by the power of the Holy Spirit. There is such an unmistakable unity of purpose and function within the Godhead. This powerful truth is reiterated time and time again when those who believe are baptized in the name of the Father, the Son, and the Holy Spirit.

Baptism becomes that public profession before the world. It's a bold and public statement: "I choose to follow Jesus Christ." It not only becomes a moment of encouragement to the believer and to the body of Christ, but it also becomes a point of accountability to the believer as well as to the church.

To the believer, baptism is a point of identification with the death, burial, and resurrection with Jesus Christ. It is a reminder of what God has done and how God has called the believer to live. It is the outward action signifying the spiritual entrance into the body of Christ.

Baptism is the first step in the long walk of discipleship. It's also a proclamation of the gospel to the lost. The baptism of the new believer is the expression what God has done in the heart and symbolized outwardly and before other believers. The picture of baptism mirrors the spiritual work of salvation.

The act of baptism is a gospel proclamation. How Believer's baptism by immersion places a person in the water. The individual is lowered beneath the surface of the water, picturing the spiritual death that has occurred due to sin. Then the person is raised back up signifying the raising up to spiritual life by Jesus Christ.

Though baptism is symbolic, there is a definite connection between the act of baptism and the reality of salvation. The new believer is raised to walk in newness of life, symbolizing resurrection to life while picturing the washing away of sins. When a believer is baptized, he or she is saying, "I have trusted in Jesus Christ and He has saved me and given me life. I am now a child of God and a follower of Jesus Christ." At this point there is a mutual accountability between the new believer and other believers in the church.

To the church, baptism of the new believer is the signal to finish the commission of Jesus Christ by "teaching (the new believer) to observe all that Jesus has commanded." This part is crucial and if the church is to make disciples, this teaching of obedience cannot be overlooked or the task has not been finished.

In the late 1900s there were various programs brought forth to encourage and teach the believers how to share their faith. This era was beneficial to the church. These programs helped the church to proclaim the gospel message to a lost world.

However, many of these programs only addressed part of the problem. Proclamation is only the beginning of the process of teaching obedience to the believer. Discipleship involves the whole process from proclamation to Christian maturity. The believer comes into the church to be discipled and taught what it means to follow Christ. As the believer matures, the teaching of the Great Commission is that this believer is now to go and make disciples as well—to take the message of what Jesus has done, give that message to others, and then help those who receive that good news to grow in Christ. That's how all of the Great Commission is accomplished.

Here is where the church can miss the point if we are not careful. We can focus on the decision to follow Christ and miss that the decision is merely the beginning of the process, not the end. Without continued discipleship believers will often be slow to mature, leaving churches filled with immature Christians who do not exemplify the sacrificial nature of Jesus.

In order to fulfill the Great Commission, we must join with the Spirit of God in bringing all believers to Christian maturity. How else will those individuals ever enter into the life-giving task of making disciples?

The question has eternal implications for the church: "Are we making disciples?" But it's a question not left just for the church *corporately*, but also for every *individual* follower of Christ. Every believer has the responsibility to disciple. Each believer has been given the command to go and make disciples of all the nations, teaching them to obey all things as Jesus has commanded. If we neglect this God-given calling, then we enter into disobedience. Are we willing to understand and engage in what it means to make disciples? The next chapter begins to unpack *how* you can make a disciple, but before you can go make one, there has to be a self-evaluation of sorts. Let us begin by answering a key question that will become a theme in this book: How will you ever go and make disciples if you are unwilling to be one?

QUESTIONS FOR REFLECTION:

- In your own words, what is the message of the church?
- How has someone positively invested in your life? How can you do the same for someone else?
- What are some things that stand in the way of you following God? Why are they there? How can you remove them?

CHALLENGE:

As you contemplate what it means to be a disciple, talk to other people in your church who are seeking to follow Jesus. Ask them if they have been discipled or are in the process of discipling someone. Begin to get a clear picture of what is happening around you spiritually.

Chapter 2

Be One, Make One

IN ORDER TO MAKE ONE, YOU MUST BE ONE. LET that thought simmer for a while. Reflect on who you are as a disciple of Christ. The title of this book contains two words: "go" and "disciple." Go implies movement. You must go to people. Disciple carries with it the weight of an identity. It's who you are. Disciples go. They go to people. It's part of who they are. So, where are you going today?

There are thousands of people groups who have no viable access to the gospel. God continues to call people to take His message to those who have never heard. Thankfully, many respond with a "yes." With all those who go, have you ever wondered how many of the called do not go? For one reason or another there is an excuse or disqualification that keeps them from following God. Gospel disobedience is tragic.

Complacency is just as bad. Many American Christians have become so complacent that they will not take the time to share with their neighbors, their coworkers, or even their family members. Does the church care about the lost and the command of the Lord to go to them? The heart of Jesus Christ is to seek and to save the lost, and it should be the heart of everyone who has been changed by the power of the gospel. Yet for many in the church today, it is not. So what is the real problem?

One answer is that many in the church are not being challenged to live out the gospel and grow as believers. This challenge to live and grow happens best in the context of discipleship. Could it be that the church is in this state because of a lack of discipleship?

I have asked this simple question in a group setting on a number of occasions: "How many of you have ever been discipled by another more mature Christian?" The answer is always astounding to me. Few, if any, in most groups polled were ever discipled. Discipleship is not just going to church and hearing someone preach or going to a small group setting. Those things are important and needed in the church. But discipleship involves more.

Even if you never experienced personal discipleship, the Holy Spirit is working to bring you to Christian maturity and righteousness. No Christian has an excuse in the end since the power to grow through the Holy Spirit and the Word of God also effectively works in those who believe.[6] The new or young believer can grow, but something amazing happens when one life is poured into the life of another. It is like fertilizer being applied to new grass. The strengthening process is sped up. The grass becomes vibrant and healthy. The blades become wide and strong, able to endure the summer heat.

God's plan was that the believer would encourage other believers in the context of the body of Christ. The wonderful truth is that when we come to this place of pouring ourselves into another, the body grows quickly and is able to withstand spiritual heat and spiritual storms.

As a young believer, I had always understood the idea of sharing my faith. What I did not understand was the need to pour my life into other younger believers. My first idea of what that might look like came when I was a junior in high school. A man moved to our town for work. He was introduced to a group of us guys through a church event. Immediately he began to question us about our spiritual lives. Before the night was over, he had made plans to meet with 4 of us on Thursday mornings. It only lasted a few months before he moved on, but in that time, he gave us a glimpse in what it meant to pour your life into others. He shared simple truth and just as important, he shared his life.

When discipleship occurs, both the disciple and the disciple-maker benefit. The focus is usually on the one being discipled, but the disciple-maker grows as well. God blesses both parties. The one being discipled is encouraged, and the one discipling is encouraged. Being a disciple and making a disciple thus become part of the same process. You cannot separate the two concepts. To be a disciple is to make a disciple. To make a disciple is to be a disciple. Let's explore this concept more in depth.

First, there is the continual working out of what it means to follow Christ. As you help another learn to follow Jesus in this world, then you are reminded of those same truths. As you work through struggles of the Christian life and the submission to the authority of Jesus Christ, you also will be reminded of your own struggles in life. Discipleship will remind you to be humble and realize on a regular basis that the things you are pouring into someone else are needed by you as well. Both parties come to rely on the grace of God in a fresh way.

Second, accountability becomes a beautiful reality in the one who is discipling. You realize that if you are going to teach others, then you had better be working through these things yourself and regularly letting God do His work in your life.

I have walked with many people and many groups as I have sought to disciple others. The one thing I can say unequivocally is that I have grown through the process. I remember the first group of people I took through *Go Disciple*. I was stunned as I realized what God was reminding me of through our time together. I questioned whether it was the students or myself who grew more during that time.

There have been many moments, as I was talking with someone, that God convicted me about something in my own life. Sometimes in the middle of the conversation I am praying, "Lord, help me" or "Lord, forgive me." Discipleship brings wonderful accountability and encouragement into both lives.

Before you can correctly see into someone else's life, you have to be able to see yourself correctly. I have heard it said, "If you want to fix the problems of this world, begin with yourself."

God has given us the answer to the world's problems. His name is Jesus, and His work is salvation. If there is a problem in this world, it began with sin and a fallen creation. Instead of falling into hopeless despair over the issues of this world and our own personal issues, the believer can proclaim the salvation of Jesus Christ to the world.

He who has defeated death, hell, and the grave has also given life. His life is the light of humanity. New life means a total change. So fundamental is the change that it will transform everything, from the look of a person, to what he or she says to what he or she does. Everything changes.

Salvation brings new life to the one who has believed. From that point on, God, through the work of His Holy Spirit, and in conjunction with the body of Christ, helps the believer understand what it means to follow Jesus. God is always working to bring about maturity in the believer's life, *for it is God who works in you both to will and to do for His good pleasure.* [7]

The beauty and comfort of this simple phrase teaches the believer that God is working out that which is pleasing to Him in our lives. This is God's promise to the believer.

Many find themselves in frustrating places, never understanding that their reliance is to be upon God Himself. No religious order, catechism, or act of self-reliance can accomplish what only God can do. Therefore, trust in the Lord Jesus Christ takes the form of simple agreement with God. When God speaks, we listen. When God points out wrong, we agree. When He encourages moving on, then "Yes, Lord" is our answer. So the whole work of making disciples begins with you being one. It is, at its very beginning, a work that God does in us that will lead us to help others move into joyful obedience.

There is no doubt that God gives us the *desire* to do His will. But He does not stop with desire. He also gives us the *strength*—His strength—to do His will. When one believer is pouring into the life of another believer, the Lord strengthens the both of them. If the Lord works in the believer, then why do many never move on to Christian maturity and bear much fruit?

First, there is the possibility of no relationship with Jesus Christ. Going to church does not grant salvation. Claiming the label "Christian" does not save. God's grace is not genetic; it doesn't pass down from parents to children. None of these bring salvation. Salvation only comes through grace by faith in the Lord Jesus Christ. Jesus told His disciples that repentance and remission of sins should be preached in His name to all nations.

Notice the word repentance. All too often, preaching focuses on the grace of God, the mercy of God, and the goodness of God. Those are wonderful truths. Too often, however, repentance is left out. The idea of repentance is one that causes people to be uncomfortable. . . and for good reason.

The Westminster Shorter Catechism states repentance occurs when "a sinner, out of a true sense of his sin, and apprehension of the mercy of God in Christ, doth, with grief and hatred of his sin, turn from it unto God, with full purpose of, and endeavor after, new obedience"[8]

It is much more than just agreeing that Jesus offered salvation to humanity through His life, death, and resurrection. Many who frequent the church are religious in an outward sense, but their religion is not true. It is based on a lie and assumption that good church attendance leads to life, when in fact the only hope is by faith in the Lord Jesus Christ.

Without repentance, then we're like the Pharisees in the Bible. The Pharisees of Jesus' day were condemned by the Lord as "white washed tombs" meaning they looked clean on the outside, but on the inside they were full of death. They were actually rejecting God the Father by rejecting God the Son. Do not be caught in the same lie. No person can work for salvation. Self-reliance leads only to arrogant self-righteousness.

Second, another reason why people do not mature is the lack of Great Commission obedience. Jesus said to "Go therefore and make disciples of all the nations, baptizing them in the name of the Father and of the Son and of the Holy Spirit, teaching them to observe all things that I have commanded you."

Following baptism we are to teach people to observe

Jesus' commandments. This teaching is another aspect of discipleship. The word "observe" means to keep or watch carefully. In this context we are to keep and watch carefully the commands that Jesus Christ has given.

The simple answer to why Christians do not grow is a lack of obedience to Jesus' Great Commission. When I was a young man, I distinctly heard the call of God at the age of twelve. I knew that I was lost and needed salvation. Sensing my burden, my father came to me one evening and said, "Son, when God calls you, obey Him immediately. It does not matter what is going on or where you find yourself. Just obey."

I took those words to heart, as I sat in church the next Sunday. My dad pastored a small church in the mountains of North Georgia. It was a beautiful sunny morning. My father had been preaching for ten minutes when I knew I had to do something. I tugged on the sleeve of my mother and told her I needed to go forward. Surprised, she asked, "Now?"

"Yes!" was my answer.

I went forward, and the service immediately changed. The Sunday service had been interrupted by the salvation of God!

At the age of sixteen I distinctly heard God call me again. This time His call was for me to preach. I was scared and tried to run from God's call. I ran far and wide trying to fill my life with things that would satisfy. Fast-forward a few years later and I found myself in church with a young lady, Heather, who would eventually become my beautiful wife. I began to grow again under the preaching of Johnny Hunt. He was fiery and taught with conviction and power.

He was preaching through the book of James and came to the passage in chapter four: "Draw near to me and I will draw near to you. Cleanse your hands you sinners and purify your hearts you double-minded." In that moment, I wanted to draw near to God, but I had to come to the reality that I had been disobedient. These words came to heart. "You can never move past the point of disobedience." At that moment, I knew that I needed to confess my sin, repent, and turn to God in obedience.

After that confession, I began to grow at a rapid pace. My faith was strengthened. The only difference was a heart of obedience.

Disobedience always leads to a break in fellowship between God and people. The disobedient heart desires to go its own way and have its own will. This is the way of the "flesh," as the Apostle Paul calls it. He would even say, "For I know that in me (that is, in my flesh) nothing good dwells."[9] If nothing good dwells there, then how foolish would it be to follow the leading of the flesh in this life. Disobedience destroys fellowship, but it also leads to destruction. When we sin against God, our wage is death.

Sin leads to death, but faith in Jesus Christ leads to eternal life. Where there is life there will be growth. When one comes to faith in Jesus Christ, he receives forgiveness and eternal life. New life leads to growth and that growth is what the Bible calls *sanctification*. The word means to be consecrated and made holy. God takes the new creation and begins His work of life in the individual. Over time, the life that has been changed grows and matures, becoming more reflective of Jesus Christ. This is because new life has its birth in the Spirit of God.

A person born of the Spirit of God is a child of God. Since we are His children, we become heirs of God in Jesus. If I live in obedience to God, it is because I am His child. Teaching a believer to obey all things as Jesus has commanded is to simply help the child of God act and live like it.

It is precious beyond words when a believer takes what God has done in his or her life and steps into the life of another and begins to model obedience. We become the living example of Jesus in the life of another. It is a natural progression in the growth of a believer.

I remember the first time I began to disciple someone intentionally. I had been walking with the Lord for a short time, and a group of four college guys asked me to disciple them. I had no idea what to do, but I took the time on Saturday mornings to spend with them, and we went through the book of John. I remember the feeling of being obedient to God. It was good and right. It filled me with the kind of joy that makes you want more of it. What little I felt I had, I chose to give to others and God greatly blessed it.

QUESTIONS FOR REFLECTION:

- Do you have a *relationship* with Jesus Christ?
- In what areas of your life are you living in obedience?
- What part of you is most susceptible to disobedience? How can you prevent falling into disobedience?
- Are you neglecting God's calling in any way? How have you neglected it?
- Are you representing Jesus Christ in your daily life with your family, friends, and the people you come in contact with each day?

CHALLENGE:

Are you willing to be used by God to change someone else's life? If so, ask God to help you submit in a greater way. If you have been walking with the Lord for a long time or a short time, today is a new day and it can lead to greater submission to the Lord. Open your heart to what God is speaking to you and agree with Him in it.

CHAPTER 3

The Disciple

"A DISCIPLE IS A FOLLOWER OF JESUS CHRIST." At least that was the statement I grew up hearing. It's true enough. However, as time moves on things change. One instance is in language. Over time words tend to change and meanings tend to shift.

For example, the word "awful" has completely changed its meaning. Noah Webster's 1828 Dictionary states the definition of "awful" as "That strikes with awe; that fills with profound reverence; as the awful majesty of Jehovah"[10] In the 19th century that was the common use for the word. Today, if I were to tell you that the food I had just eaten was awful, you would not think it "inspired a sense of awe."

Another word that has expanded in meaning in the 21st century is the word "follower." The definition of "follower" is "one in the service of another, one that follows the opinions or teachings of another, or one that imitates another."[11]

However, social media has helped reshape the meaning of "follower." At the time of this writing, I am pleased to announce I am "following" 55 people and 93 people are "following" me. . . on Twitter. In this context, the word "follower" means "someone who watches for pithy statements of the one that is being followed." So, "follow" now equates with general observance. If we take that definition of "following" and apply it, then one will find much of modern-day Western Christianity fits this definition of "following" Jesus Christ. There is an outward general expression of interest in the teaching of Jesus. There may even be a sense of devotion to Him, as shown in church attendance or benevolent acts.

Many who claim to be Christians are simply followers in the sense that they are general observers to Jesus Christ. I am positive that this is not what Jesus had in mind when He looked out and said, "If anyone desires to follow me." Because of this, there is some need to define discipleship in the context of being follower of Jesus Christ. Let us start with what we know about being a disciple.

First, we know the definition of the word in the original language of the New Testament simply means "a learner, or one who is instructed."[12] There is a relationship between the one who teaches and the one who is being taught. Inherent in the relationship is the imparting of knowledge to the disciple. This means there has to be willingness and humility that allows the disciple to be taught.

One time, I was taking a small group through *Go Disciple* and one of the participants was a mature Christian whom I had known for years. She was older than me, and I respected her greatly. In fact, I was a bit intimidated and thought, "What can I teach her?"

As we got deep into discussion around the fourth week of meeting, she came in and she was broken. I remember thinking, "Oh Lord, I have messed this lady up." But, as we began to talk, she started unfolding the amazing work that God had been doing in her life. Part of it had to do with submitting to teaching and ultimately submitting to God. What had happened is that she had humbled herself before God, letting me teach, and God began to show her things that she needed to deal with in her own life.

If part of following Jesus is learning, then we have to humble ourselves and be teachable. A disciple is someone who is learning.

The next part of discipleship is modeling what is taught. Here is where knowledge comes alive in the face of everyday life and situations. This is the point where what is learned comes to guide and direct the disciple's life. It is one thing to be taught something by hearing it, but how much more impactful is it to be taught something and then see it modeled in life.

As a young couple, my wife and I felt that God was leading us to go to school and continue in ministry. We would term it "the great adventure" and move to another state, leaving jobs and family. I eventually finished my Master's Degree and went on to work with college students.

At one point I remember looking back over my hard earned degree and thinking, "Am I using anything I learned in those years?" The answer was a resounding "Yes!" The education had expanded my mind and given me a foundation for ministry, preaching, counseling, and administration within the church. What I was having a problem with was applying that day to day. What I needed was someone to show me how to do it. I began listening and watching those who were a little further down the road in ministry, and it made all the difference in the world.

I had learned a lot of knowledge, but what impacted me was watching those things I had learned be applied in everyday life. All of the sudden the knowledge came alive. I just needed help to see it.

That is what is so amazing about Jesus. He didn't just tell us what to do. He showed us how to do it. He lived it out so we can live it out. Added to that is the gift of the

Holy Spirit to empower us to get it done and guide us. So when Jesus said, "If anyone desires to follow me," He is not offering mere head knowledge, but a complete change of life through what He has modeled.

To go and make disciples means to share the truth of what God has done in giving salvation to us through the blessed, holy, and perfect work of Jesus Christ. Then baptize them in the name of the holy and triune God. But the Great Commission does not stop there. We must teach them to observe or keep all things as Jesus has command-ed. If that were not enough, Jesus goes on to tell those first disciples that, "as you go and make disciples, do not worry for I (Jesus) am with you even to the end."

Jesus is saying to the first disciples that "I was with you to teach you, and I will not leave you nor forsake you" in the mission that I am giving you. What a comforting thought to those whose lives had just been radically clarified. One of the most comforting passages the believer could ever understand is Galatians 4:6-7: "And because you are sons, God has sent forth the Spirit of His Son into your hearts, crying out, "Abba, Father!" Therefore you are no longer a slave but a son, and if a son, then an heir of God through Christ."

This is the fulfillment of what Jesus said to the disciples in John 14 when the Spirit of Truth was promised: "I will not leave you orphans; I will come to you." This glorious truth is a comfort to the disciple and is bound by the words of the Savior Himself and sealed in eternity. The disciples had been taught by the Lord Jesus for three years and now would be given the Spirit of God Himself. All of that teaching would now be brought to life in the soul of the disciples, enabling them to fulfill the commission that had been given to them.

The teaching and empowering of God would be the only way that these early disciples could go and fulfill the mission that Jesus had given them. It was God who directed them, empowered them, and had them write the letters that would change lives all over the world.

Through those few early disciples, God would change the world. The gospel would be taken to the uttermost parts of the world, and even now we have a chance to be a part of God's unfolding plan of salvation to the nations.

Surely a disciple is more than a mere follower as we define the term today. Many had followed Jesus because of what He had done. The facts are that He did some amazing things in a public way, like turning water into wine and feeding five thousand at one time. Because of these incredible acts, some followed Him in amazement. The tragedy is that they should have been following Him for who He was, not only for what He did.

In John 6, Jesus plainly reveals who He is and what it would take to follow Him. The difficulty of what He teaches would be captured in the actions of the many would-be followers with these words, "From that time many of His disciples went back and walked with Him no more." Many followed at a distance, but when confronted with the reality of what it would really mean to follow Him, they turned back.

How sad it is—the abundant life that only God Himself can give is forsaken. And the opportunity to be used by God in a life-changing and world-shaking way is forfeited because of a choice not to walk closely as His disciple. If one will not be a disciple then how will he or she ever go and make disciples?

Another aspect of being a follower is surrendering. A disciple of Jesus Christ is one who is surrendered and submitted to His Lordship, seeking to follow His life and teaching with a willingness to do whatever God asks. The disciple is always seeking to learn and apply.

If you are willing to be devoted to following Jesus, then you will inherently be led to make disciples. The disciple maker is always pointing the one who is being discipled to Jesus Christ while modeling the Christian life by the power of the Holy Spirit.

The beauty is that as we go and make disciples, we are continually pointing to Jesus Christ in our teaching and in the way we live our lives. One truth that will quickly be discovered is that in this process the disciple makers are reminded of all that they have learned, and a beautiful accountability arises naturally within the discipling relationship. The blessing is reciprocal.

Faith-empowered obedience will show where our allegiance lies. Jesus said, "If you love me, keep My commandments. . . He who does not love Me does not keep My words." That pretty much sums it up. If the believer professes a love for Jesus Christ, then there will be obedience. If there is no love for the Savior, then there will be no obedience.

Do you profess a love for the Lord? If so, does that love express itself in love-filled obedience that is full of grace and truth? That is a question for each member of the church. And what is indicative of each member of a church will be indicative of that church as a whole. If the people of God confess the great confession, "Jesus Christ is Lord," then obedience should follow.

The truth is that many churches grow cold and cease to make any impact in this world, simply because they have forgotten what it means to obey. If obedience has been discarded, it can mean only one thing. Their love for God has gone cold as well. If you love Jesus, then you will keep His commandments.

The effects of loveless Christians and the churches they frequent are all around us. They lack a holy presence in the public square. They do not stand for truth. Has the church forgotten her first love? Is there no hope? With all my heart and soul the Spirit of God rises within me to say, "There is a hope!" Because God is calling this generation back to Himself as He has done with the generations of the past. God is calling us back to love and obedience and to take hold of His life-changing message. May it take hold of us that we might go and give it to others.

Let the church of Jesus Christ rise and finish the task that was started over 2,000 years ago. Let her be a people who make disciples intent on going to make more disciples. It can happen, and it begins with you. Jesus said, "If anyone desires to come after me. . ." This is where it begins. You have to come to the place where you are willing to commit and give your life to follow Jesus. It is where you get in line right behind Him and go where He goes and do what He does. If you do, be sure that the Spirit of God will strengthen you and empower you to do that which is impossible for us alone. He will help you to become a disciple who will *go disciple.*

Questions for reflection:

- Describe what the life of a disciple might look like in today's context.
- Do you love God above all things?
- Do you love others above yourself?
- How might your day look different if God were first?
- How might your day look different in your relationships toward others if you loved others like Jesus loves them?

Challenge:

Do you submit to biblical teaching in your life? Notice I did not ask if you go to church or are involved in a small group. By "submitted" I mean do you yield or agree with someone speaking into your life? Do you allow people to hold you accountable? Ask the Lord to search your heart concerning these things and see if He reveals any hidden pride that would keep you from following Jesus.

Chapter 4

Life

Now great multitudes went with Him. And He turned and said to them, "If anyone comes to Me and does not hate his father and mother, wife and children, brothers and sisters, yes, and his own life also, he cannot be My disciple. And whoever does not bear his cross and come after Me cannot be My disciple. For which of you, intending to build a tower, does not sit down first and count the cost, whether he has enough to finish it— lest, after he has laid the foundation, and is not able to finish, all who see it begin to mock him, saying, 'This man began to build and was not able to finish'? Or what king, going to make war against another king, does not sit down first and consider whether he is able with ten thousand to meet him who comes against him with twenty thousand? Or else, while the other is still a great way off, he sends a delegation and asks conditions of peace. So likewise, whoever of you does not forsake all that he has cannot be My disciple.

Luke 14:25-33

AT A FIRST GLANCE THIS PASSAGE IS DISTURB-ing. At a second and deeper glance, it might become even more disturbing. Jesus is confronting the idea that you can have this world and all that it offers while following Him with sincerity of heart. No heart can have two loves. You can't love Jesus and at the same time love the ways of the world. They are diametrically opposed.

Jesus demonstrates that *no man can serve two masters for he will love the one and hate the other or hate the one and love the other.* Simply, the human heart has the capacity to worship in only one direction. Anything else is self-serving hypocrisy. The sad news is we're all guilty. We have all tried to love in the wrong way.

Jesus says, "If anyone comes to Me, and does not hate his Father, mother, wife, children brothers and sisters and his own life also cannot be my disciple." In a startling statement that is both clear and concise, Jesus confronts the hands-off distant approach to following Him.

Notice that *a great multitude followed Him.* There are great multitudes of would-be followers who claim Jesus, whether they are culturally Christian by social grouping or regularly attend church. To these and the rest of the disciples Jesus says something that will destroy the myth that one can follow Jesus in a halfhearted, distant manner. "If anyone comes to me and does not *hate* his father and mother, wife and children, brothers and sisters, yes, and his own life also, he cannot be My disciple" (emphasis mine).

Is Jesus commanding hatred? If so, this is directly in contrast to His other teachings. Jesus had taught His disciples that if one had anger in his heart then it was the same as murder in the heart. The Apostle John would go on to say, "Whoever hates his brother is a murderer." [13]

So what is He saying? Jesus is not commanding hatred. On the contrary, He is demanding allegiance and surrender. He turns to the large crowd that is following Him and He makes a point that is so striking and disturbing to the masses that it becomes undeniable. He reveals that they either stand as distant followers or close disciples.

Jesus is telling all those who would follow Him that compared to the love they have for their own family, their love and desire to follow Him should be deeper. The contrast here is deep as He calls to the would-be follower, "There is no relationship in this world that is to be before your relationship with Me." If there is a relationship that comes before Him, then how will you be a sold-out follower? The other relationship will sooner or later interfere in your relationship to Christ.

At times this tragically lived out in the church. A believer is not to be yoked together with an unbeliever, as Paul would tell the Corinthian church. [14] Some time ago I counseled a young woman who was in a relationship with a man who was not a believer. The counsel was that she should not be in the relationship because Scripture expressly spoke against it. What communion has light with darkness? She would not listen and gave excuse after excuse as to why she should remain in the relationship. In the end, she did not listen. The relationship drew her away from fellowship with God and with the body of Christ.

The worldly relationship had led her away from following the Lord. In my own life I have had to confront this same thinking. Years ago I felt that God was leading me to take a trip overseas to share the gospel in Eastern Europe. My wife, Heather, and I had just had our first son. Before I left on the trip I had this fear that I was going to die. I did not want to leave my wife and my son. The fear seemed to grip my heart. I boarded the plane, buckled up and thought, "I am going to die on this trip." As the plane ascended through the clouds, I began praying and said, "Lord I am willing to die for you." At that moment, God spoke to my heart with unmistakable clarity saying, "Good, now that you will die for me, go live for me." It was like a light bulb came on, and I understood that to live for Jesus was to give up my life. I was not losing anything. I was simply giving up less for more. What I really found was that Jesus offers more life, more joy, and more fulfillment. It was one of those moments that was life-changing and life-altering. I have never forgotten that moment and pray I never do.

I ended up having a wonderful trip sharing the gospel and preaching in churches in that formerly communist country. I returned home alive physically, but inside I knew something had changed.

Although I did not die, I must be willing to die and count myself as dead already. Loving God more than trying to hold on to my family was important in leading me to understand what He would say next in this passage: "If anyone comes to Me and does not hate. . . his own life also, he cannot be My disciple."

To follow Christ and become a disciple means that in contrast to loving God one must hate even his or her own life. This is being willing to give up all to follow Christ.

Let me pose an important question: What is assumed in "life"? I asked a small group of students we were discipling this same question. Those students began to discuss the concept of life. As the conversation progressed you could see a look of fear first, which quickly turned into a realization concerning the state of their hearts. Our lives consist of all that we are—past and present. If a follower desires to be a disciple, all that is assumed in life must be given to Jesus. That involves our past and our present, but where we struggle is the thought of giving up our future. Life consists of the whole, and the whole belongs to God if we are to follow Him.

Most young people want to have a family. I have found

that young women particularly struggle in this area. I have watched young ladies deal with their own desire to have families and come to a place where they can give up all those dreams to follow the Lord. The Lord in His perfect love and gentleness brings them to a place where they can surrender to His Lordship, and the Lord sets them free. Instead of being bound by what they think "should be," they come to a place of surrender to God's will.

The desire to marry and have a family is not inherently bad. What God requires is that the desire for family does not come before our desire for Him. Most will marry and have families, and some will not. No matter the state you find yourself in, the truth is that God is the only one who can ultimately fulfill and give lasting satisfaction.

Now the same principle is true for those who have families. My love and desire for God should be above all things. My desire to honor God will lead me to love, honor, and sacrifice for my wife. My first place love for God will lead me to be a father who desires to raise a godly heritage. Family or not, God is preeminent.

As those students continued the discussion of what life means in this passage, one young woman said, "My life is also my need for approval." When she said that statement those five students all nodded in agreement. Why do we desire approval? This question gets to the bare places of our hearts. We desire approval because when someone approves of us, they have said, "Yes, I agree with who you are and what you are doing."

I have five sons. Each one of them is a magnificent creation of God, as are all children. They are quite different, but have one common need. They all need the affirmation of their father. I have been harsh with them at times, and I have seen it crush their spirits. In those times I have had to get on a knee, look them in the eye, and say with shame in my heart, "Daddy did not represent Jesus in the way I just acted. Will you forgive me?"

On the other hand when I, by the grace of God, have handled situations correctly and affirmed my children, the response has been incredible. Even in disciplining them I try to encourage them to godliness, telling them what was wrong, how it can be made right, and to trust God for strength to live correctly.

I look at those boys and tell them, "I love you" and then ask the question, "Do you know why I love you?" They respond with a question, "Why?" My response is "Because there is only one you, and God created you amazingly!" They light up. We all need affirmation. We all want to be loved and thought of well.

One afternoon I stopped at a convenience store for a drink. I walked up to the counter and put the drink on the counter as I pulled out my wallet. This lady looked aged beyond her years. It looked like she had had a rough life, and she looked tired. As she finished, she asked if I needed anything else. I responded, "No ma'am. That will do it." She immediately responded with, "Don't call me ma'am, I am not that old." I responded just as quickly back, saying, "It has nothing to do with your age, you are a lady and I was being polite." She blushed at the compliment and became soft spoken in return. How long had it been or had she ever been called a lady. I meant what I said to her and she knew it. A simple affirmation had completely changed her disposition.

What if no other person on this earth ever gives you affirmation again? That would be a harsh existence. But, before our desire for affirmation from others, we must understand and receive affirmation from God. One of the first verses our children learned early was Psalm 139:14: "I praise you because I am fearfully and wonderfully made; your works are wonderful, I know that full well." I want our children to know the affirming knowledge of God's love.

The fact is that God created you. And if He created you, then He must have had a reason for doing so. If you were created for a reason, then you have purpose. If you have purpose, then you must have meaning. You were meant to have a relationship with God!

The foundational truth of our lives is that God affirms us in that He loves us with a perfect love. In discussing this truth with a group of students early one morning, a young lady spoke up and said to the entire group, "I have had to come to a place where I believed that God loved me and it was hard for me to accept." What she was confessing was that she had lived in such a way that, in her mind, there was no way that God could love her. What she failed to understand was that her idea of love was not love at all. God's perfect love is a gift that is given—a gift given with full understanding of who we are. He loves us, even though we sin. That is the essence of grace.

Another aspect of "life" is the desire to be fulfilled. Every human has this desire. Sin has ripped part of us away and left us unfulfilled. Our relationship with God was destroyed because of our own rebellion and turning away from God. That has left humanity in a state of wanting.

Now we seek every way under the sun to have this void filled. If you can name it, we have tried it. When we desire satisfaction, the underlying cause is the desire to be fulfilled.

Men can look to be fulfilled by lustful desires, by having more material possessions, or by having more power. It is scary to see a man's capacity to grow in the area of desire.

What starts as a desire to steal a candy bar from a store is the same desire that will rob a bank. This is also seen in the area of lust. What begins as a desire to look at a picture of a woman leads a man deeper into lust. Unchecked lust will lead to acting out of that lust.

On the other hand, when one begins a new life in Christ, sins are cast off in obedience and love for God. Obedience to God brings a greater appetite to do His will. The desire grows to a point that a man or woman can sell everything, leave everything they know, and live in an international culture to share the gospel with lost people.

There is no doubt that our desires and appetites grow. The question then becomes what do you desire? Is the desire of your heart leading you to a place of God's ultimate glory, a place in which the rewards are eternal and unimaginable? If not, now is a good time to come to that realization. Let's look further into the Luke 14 passage: "If anyone comes to me and does not hate. . . his own life also, he cannot be My disciple."

The would-be disciple comes to Christ alone. He brings no one else and has counted all things as loss for the sake of knowing Christ. Compared to love for Christ, the disciple hates his own life. How sad it is to see those who would grasp for their own lives in the end lose them. Does not Jesus say that anyone who loses his or her life for His sake will in the end have it? In the end, the only way to have life is to forget yours and receive His. Thus, the one who understands this is the only one who can truly live.

It is the only way to be a disciple. If you will not lay down your life, then you will never take up your cross and go on to follow Him. You must come to the place of absolute surrender.

To the carnal ear, following Jesus may sound impossible or maybe not worth the cost. But the one who comes to understand this truth in light of eternity will quickly see that the upfront cost of following Christ pales in comparison to what He offers us. You might think you are giving up something at the beginning, but in the end you will say like the Apostle Paul: "Yet indeed I also count all things loss for the excellence of the knowledge of Christ Jesus my Lord, for whom I have suffered the loss of all things, and count them as rubbish, that I may gain Christ."[15]

Friend, He is worth anything that you might be holding on to at this moment. Let your fear of giving everything up to the God—who never leaves nor forsakes—be replaced by a faith in the God who is calling to you in love.

Questions for reflection:

- What kind of things do you personally look to for fulfillment?
- What kind of things do others look to for fulfillment?
- Is God revealing things that stand in the way of following Him? If so, what are they? How is God removing these things?

Challenge:

Spend time contemplating what it means to surrender. Ask God to reveal any areas of your life that are not surrendered. Write them down and lay them out before God seeking His help in surrendering.

CHAPTER 5

God Pursues

THE DESIRE TO KNOW GOD IS A MIRACLE IN itself. A quick glance through the Bible will illustrate the point. Adam and Eve sinned against God in a garden where there was perfect harmony and peace. They had such an intimate relationship with their Creator that He *walked in the garden with them and spoke with them.*[16] When Adam allowed sin into their lives everything changed. They were corrupted, and their relationship with their Creator was broken. From that point on, humanity turned away from God.

When God says that *all have sinned and fallen short of His glory,* He is speaking of all humanity. That is the state in which we all find ourselves outside of salvation in Jesus Christ.

This one fact will clear up the question that is heard so often by those who struggle with an omnipotent and sovereign God. That question is "If God is all powerful, then why does He let bad things happen?" This sounds like a good question but it comes from a wrong perspective. This question assumes that humanity is good and this world is good.

On the other hand, when we come from the perspective that all humanity has rejected God and therefore rejected true love, righteousness, holiness, and essential goodness, the question then becomes how does anything good happen in this world? Humanity chose to sin and that sin, which is rejection of God, had consequences which were cosmic in nature. When Adam sinned, he took creation with Him.

When humanity turned from God in the garden, people turned to death and destruction. Never underestimate the destructive power of sin. Every time you hear of war, killing, destruction of lives, or abuse of children, remember it is a product of humanity's rebellion. Let it cause you to hate sin with passion, a hatred that is only exceeded by your love for God.

Genesis 3 records the sad words of Adam and Eve's Creator walking in the cool of the day and the couple hiding among the trees. God calls out to them, "Where are you?" This is an interesting question for a couple of reasons.

One is, "I am looking for you and you are not here with me." The second is, "Do you know where you are?" Instead of walking in fellowship, they are hiding in fear among the creation. The garden was a place to commune with one another and to walk with their God in fellowship. Now the creation had become a hiding place to get away from God because the perfect fellowship had been broken.

God confronts their hiding, and then He confronts the fact that they tried to cover themselves to hide from one another. Their relationship was broken. Everything changed, and from that moment until now we see God coming not just to walk in fellowship, but also to restore fellowship. The stories of God coming to humanity in Scriptures are so numerous that this fact alone gives us a clue to what the entire Bible is about.

In Genesis 5 God speaks to Noah and reveals He is going

to destroy the earth. Then Noah obeys God and builds the ark that would save his family. The Lord came to Abram in Genesis 12 and said, "Go from your country and your kindred and your father's house to the land that I will show you. And I will bless you and make you a great nation." In response, Abram believed God.

Later in Abram's life God would visit him and make a covenant that would lead to the fulfillment of the promise God had earlier made. In making the covenant, God changed the name of Abram, meaning "exalted father," to Abraham, which means "father of a multitude." Through-out the rest of the Bible there is this beautiful theme of God confronting, visiting, and guiding His people to salvation.

This all leads to the most fantastic event in the history of creation. Something so radical and "other" that the thought is almost incomprehensible. The Creator comes to be a part of creation. Now God is not only visiting humanity, He has become man. And He did it perfectly.

Now the Just One goes even further by going to the cross and taking the penalty for the sins of humanity. He paid no penalty for Himself. Rather, he became sin so we might become the righteousness of God in Him.[17] The first Adam failed and sinned, being the head of the fallen race of humanity. This second Adam, Jesus Christ, would be the head of a new line of redeemed men and women. Forever purchased from the slavery of death and transferred into the kingdom of the Son of God's love.

It is God who has sought us. And it is an act of God that we desire to come after Him. He is, after all, the Author and Finisher of our faith. In Christ, our lack of holiness is con-sumed by His eternal holiness, and those who would come to Him in faith are given what He has secured. The ques-tion then becomes, "Why would He do this for a rebellious creation?" There is only one answer to this question: Love. Perfect love. Love as only God has it.

If you ever wanted to know what true love is, you need look no further than the work of Jesus Christ. The book of I John so beautifully expresses and explains this love. In Chapter 4 John speaks of the fact that God is love. If we do not love, then we do not know God for this God is love. Since He is perfect and true, He must act in accordance with who He is.

True love acts in the best interest of the one who is being loved, no matter what the cost. Love does not insist on its own way. Western culture has so romanticized love that it has come to be equated with a feeling. Thus the misconceptions of love abound. The ideas of "falling in and out of love" as if by chance or fate are not found in the Scriptures and are not indicative of true love.

God's love caused Him to act on behalf of the humanity that He had created. Because of His love, He sent His Son on a mission to find and save you. This salvation is the absolute picture of God's love. Jesus, being fully God and perfect man, continued to live and operate in the perfect love that was indicative of who He was, and this led Him to continue in the mission for which He was sent. That mission of love led Him to the cross—where we find the complete picture of love. Jesus offered His life up as a sacrifice for humanity. No one could take it unless He had already given it.

True love also begins with God because He is the definition of love. Therefore, God *is* love. He is the initiator of love, and if humanity is to know anything of love it is because God has revealed it. The significance of this is that humanity, in its fallen and rebellious state, has become ignorant of perfect love. Outside of God, humanity only has hints and shadows of the totality of that love.

Humanity was created with the need for love and when people do not feel and experience that love in their lives it can have destructive consequences. I was recently speaking on a retreat with young people. There was a young lady there whom I had met briefly some time ago. As we began to get into the retreat, God was opening up hearts to His truth and His love. About halfway through the retreat this young lady came and sat down beside me. Her eyes betrayed her smile, and I knew there was something deep going on in her heart. We sat there and looked out over the rolling waves lapping up on the beach. She was quiet for what seemed like five minutes. Finally, and without looking at her, I asked her what was going on.

Immediately tears came to her eyes. I knew she had a difficult family life growing up and figured it might have something to do with that situation. It did, just not the way I thought.

She began to tell me how over the past week she had been drinking a lot. At that point she began to sob. I put my arm around her, and we sat there while she cried. When she finally calmed down, she began to unfold the past week of destruction. She had woken up three times with someone different each time and did not remember how she got there any of those times. She was a wreck. The more she spoke, the more it became clear. This young lady needed love and the love she needed was not the trash she was getting from the world.

I began to speak to her as a father who loved her, cared for her, and accepted her. In those moments as I explained the perfect love of the Heavenly Father, it became so clear that the world couldn't offer what she sought. This world is filled with broken people looking for love, and they are looking for it in a world that cannot give it. Only God can give it. It is a love without error, and He desires that you experience it.

God's love is perfect and that means it is in perfect concert with all of His other attributes. His love works perfectly in the context of His justice. Therefore, the love of God is perfectly fair and judiciously flawless. When people ask the question, "Did Jesus have to die on the cross to pay the penalty for sin or could there have been some other way." The first part of that answer is, that Jesus asked if there was any other way three times in the garden. The answer from the Father was that the cross was the only way. Second, in harmony with the perfect love and justice of God, if there could have been some other way, then God would have accomplished salvation differently. Jesus perfectly paid the perfect price according to the fact that He is just and He is love. These two attributes of God were perfectly displayed in salvation.

His love works with each of His attributes in perfect harmony. The magnificence, beauty, and perfection of the Lord leads those who would contemplate the unsearchable riches in Christ Jesus our Lord to one thing: worship.

When we look to God and have nothing but awe and reverence, our hearts are changed as we are confronted with His perfect love. In this beautiful confrontation of love, we begin to understand life and what it is to live it. But even more profound than this is that sinful people who rejected God are strangely drawn to desire God. It is a miracle when a wretched sinner comes to the place where the desire for God is birthed in the heart.

If you desire God, be thankful and humbled that God would stoop down to you, humble Himself, and become obedient to death, even death on the cross. Be thankful that He would pay the penalty for your sin and offer you His righteousness in return. He is doing this that we might be saved from destruction and that we would be brought back into a relationship with our Creator. God is doing the work. He is working in us to change our hearts and then to give us the strength do that for which He is molding our hearts. For it is God who works in you both to will and to do for His good pleasure.[18]

God desires to do a work in you. Be honest with yourself and then be honest with God. Ask God to search your heart and to reveal the state of your heart. Spend time in the Bible and allow God to speak to you.

When Jesus confronts you, will your answer be "Yes, Lord"? Before you can move on to follow Christ, the question of desire must be answered. Do you desire God? If so, you are entering into the greatest journey a man or woman can know. It is not an easy journey. The price high, but the journey is sweet. And the price you pay does not even compare to the return you get. If you desire to come after the Savior, then the next step will be to deny yourself.

QUESTIONS FOR REFLECTION:

- What effect has sin had on your life?
- How has God pursued you?
- What are some ways you have pushed back against God's pursuit?
- God loves you perfectly. What impact will this truth have on the way you live?

CHALLENGE:

Spend some time paying attention to what you desire. Get your debit card statement or checkbook and see where you spend your money. It might be a good indicator of what your heart desires. Second, what do you desire in life? Ask someone close to you to answer that question for you.

CHAPTER 6

Self

A HEART THAT HAS BEEN RESHAPED TO SEEK God and His will immediately finds opposition. An immature follower of Christ is often surprised to find this opposition coming not only from without but from within.

Two general thoughts about humanity exist. The first thought is that humanity is generally good but something happened to make people do bad things. The other view is that humanity is inherently bad, and in order for us to be good there has to be some type of intervention that pushes us toward good.

Biblically speaking, humanity turned from God and is inherently corrupt at the most basic spiritual level. Practically, this can be seen in young children who can be astonishingly selfish.

When my oldest son was about three years old, I walked in the kitchen when I saw it: the startled, trying to hide something, sleight of hand move. I asked, "What are you doing?" "Nothing", he said. "Then what is behind your back?" With shame he pulled his hand from behind his back and showed me the sucker that belonged to his little brother. I assure you that I did not teach him how to steal. He figured it out all by himself. His own desire had led him to do what was wrong.

Heather and I have five boys, and each one of them can

be sinful and selfish. That may sound harsh, but remember they get it from their father. I can be selfish and sinful as anyone. Quite frankly, so can you. Unless God confronts us there can be no resolution to this problem of sin. When a believer desires to follow after Jesus Christ there will be an immediate confrontation with sinful self.

The Apostle Paul writes, "In me, that is in my flesh dwells no good thing." We are inherently sinful. If you begin from this vantage point, the landscape of humanity becomes painfully clear. A fallen and broken world will remain in this state unless confronted by His truth and righteous.

We come to the point of salvation by faith believing on the Lord Jesus and when we do the Scriptures say that we are born again. This means something new has come to be in the depths of our soul. We are a new creation in Jesus Christ. This regeneration happens at the heart level, and we are awakened by the Spirit of God through salvation in Jesus Christ, which changes us at the core of who we are, giving us life in Christ. This new life resides in this old body, which is corrupt. Now God begins to work and to give us the will to do what is good, right, and godly because we are now born in the Spirit of God thus making us children of God.

The confrontation that now takes place is the Spirit of God working in us that we might not live, walk and think in those old fleshly ways. Therefore, the Apostle Paul says walk in the Spirit that you might not fulfill the desires of the flesh. The sinful flesh of humanity is an enemy of God. This disturbing thought is the reality of humanity. If a believer does not understand this basic truth, then confusion and disillusionment are sure to follow.

It is confusing to hear the talk of being born again, of being a new creation, and salvation and then to go about your day and feel the pull of sin trying to rip you away from walking with God unless you understand that this new creation is born into this old body. Now, the Spirit of God has freed the heart and mind from the power of sin. The believer now has the ability and freedom to walk in the power of the Spirit and not fulfill the lust of the flesh.

Paul also writes, "But the natural man does not receive the things of the Spirit of God, for they are foolishness to him; nor can he know them, because they are spiritually discerned."[19] The flesh of humanity does not comprehend the things of God. It only seeks sinfully for itself and cannot be trusted. This is why it is so important to read and study the Scriptures. Understand what God has said about this struggle and do not be caught off guard.

One thing the Church must watch for is teaching a "do it yourself" gospel. The answer to the flesh is not handling it in your own power, nor is it about trying harder. On the contrary, it is about yielding to the Spirit of God. If you would, this day, yield moment by moment as the Lord prompts you, there would be the blessing of obedience to God, and you would be used as His chosen vessel to bless others.

The Religion of Self

Self is its own religion with two basic tenants. The first one is self-preservation, and the second one is self-exaltation. You could say these are two sides of the same coin of man's sinful creed.

We are inherently concerned about ourselves and what belongs to us. I asked a group of students a simple question: "What is wrapped up in 'self'"? Their answers hit right to the point and as each one spoke. Words like lust, desire, my dreams, and greed began to expose hearts. But one young woman quietly spoke up and said "fear." At that moment there was check in my spirit, and I asked her to describe what she was talking about. We sat there for a few minutes as she explained the bondage of fearing what other people thought about her, and it led her to care more about what others thought than what God thought.

Most of us struggle at some point with this fear. What is at the heart of this sin might surprise you. It is nothing more than pride. Fear of man will drive you into a protective state. What we are protecting is *self.* This is pride. We fear what people will think and what people will say. This causes us to react in unhealthy and sinful ways. It would be easy at this point to believe that we are putting others before God and stop there. While it is true that we often care more about what people say than God, the heart of this issue is that the fear is about "self." It is what people "think of *me*" or "how they perceive *me.*"

Self is actually the culprit. Our desire to be accepted, loved and wanted has been subverted by sin. For example, when we fear man, we are actually protecting *self.* This explains the power of peer pressure. We end up living in a prison of what we think we should be from other people's perspective. *Self* will never be satisfied and always striving for more approval, leading to an endless spiral of desperation and ending in bitterness of perceived failure.

Self-exaltation

The other side of the coin is self-exaltation. It cannot be disconnected from self-preservation. In self-exaltation, *self* sits upon a temporary and wicked throne. There is only one who is worthy of honor and praise. It's not you. It's not me.

In the throne room of Heaven, John saw the acts and

words of worship when he saw the twenty-four elders fall down before Him who sits on the throne and worship Him who lives forever and ever, and cast their crowns before the throne, saying: "You are worthy, O Lord, To receive glory and honor and power; For You created all things, And by Your will they exist and were created."[20] The description of the throne room is shocking itself. Yet it is incomparable to the One who sits on the throne. Man's only response to the awesome presence of God is fall down before Him and cast the crowns of exaltation before the only One worthy of exaltation. The word *cast* means to let go of something and not care where it lands.

The problem with sinful *self* is that it casts no crown in humble adoration before God. In our sinfulness the desire is to be lifted and exalted instead of exalting God. This is the heart of evil itself and it is the heart of an unredeemed person. We do not want God's way. The natural self definitely does not desire to bow before His will or give up everything that defines us.

Therefore, if the natural man desires to exalt *self* before God then you better believe that your desire to exalt self is above others as well. This leads to broken relationships. Most likely, all of us have been a part of a broken relationship, whether it is a friend, classmate, coworker, sibling, parent, or even a spouse. The effects of these broken relationships tend to have a devastating consequence on our lives.

There is a term used in some cases of marital divorce called, "irreconcilable differences." The term is used for what courts call a "no-fault" divorce in which the couple believes that to continue in the marriage is impossible. The heart of the issue is one of reconciliation. One or both in the marriage are unwilling to yield to the other or to forgive the other.

What if both people in the marriage humbled themselves with an open heart, asked for forgiveness and offered forgiveness? Could a marriage be saved? Could a home remain intact and find healing? Absolutely! However, this will never happen when *self* sinfully remains in control.

At the root of self-preservation and self-exaltation is pride, and pride is deceptively evil. Pride is nothing more than empty self-assurance. Pride leads one to think "I can do *it* in my own power," or "I can trust in my own ability and resources." Pride stands in the face of God and says, "I do not need You." Pride is a lie, and at its end is destruction because at its heart is rejection of God and His way.

The Answer to the Problem of Self

Self-based pride is a lie. The way to confront a lie is to confront it with truth. Truth has its foundation in the One from whom truth emanates. God is truth, so what He reveals to us will be truth.

It is also true that God is love, as I John shows us. From that love flows God's grace and mercy. From grace and mercy flows God's beautiful and humbling forgiveness. That you and I could reject God choose the side of selfishness and evil against Him is terrible. But it's more stunning that the One we rejected and opposed would come after us and give His life for us! That is what God has done for you.

Humanity is confronted by the grace of God and we stand with dirty hearts and stained hands bearing our guilt before the magnificent and holy Creator. Not all confrontation is bad. If we are wrong and confronted by what is right, then the confrontation is good. God—in His infinite goodness—confronts us who are under ultimate judgment and through Jesus Christ offers complete forgiveness.

We would be utter fools to deny His mercy and grace. When God confronts and people respond in faith everything changes. Now, through Jesus, the relationship between the Creator and His creation is restored. God and humanity can now walk together again.

Salvation comes and the Holy Spirit given life comes forth from the grave of sin and with it is birthed the desire to follow God. Now Jesus calls to the believer "Follow Me." To the one who desires to follow Him He says, "Deny yourself, take up your cross and follow me. "

Deny Self

Back to the question posed to the students, "What is wrapped up in self?" Their answers were lust, desires for self-gratification, having their own way, and a number of other answers. But in the end all of their answers led to the heart of the issue. The answer to "What is wrapped up in self?" is "me." I am wrapped up and have this fleshly tendency to make life all about me. Humanity is wrapped up in selfish pride, and it is a worship problem.

For the believer there is a call to deny this sinful self and follow Christ. At this point it might seem Jesus is calling the would-be disciple to a life of self-discipline. While there is an element of discipline in being a disciple, it more than outward conformity to a set of principles or rules.

Humanity has this incredible tendency to confuse religious rules for true worship. There is a desire to become more holy by doing and to please God by accomplishing. With that heart there is no end to our work. The vanity of such a religious system becomes a prison of expectation and never-ending guilt. This is a form of pride as well. For people to think that God is impressed by mere outward actions is foolish. This type of religion must be denied because it steals from the glory of God by saying people are capable of coming to God in their own strength. If a person, in his or her own power can come to God, then the work of Jesus on the cross is cheapened and that means the holiness of God is thereby cheapened as well.

The people of Israel had this problem. In the first chapter of Isaiah, God speaks through the prophet and tells the people to bring *no more futile offerings*. . . outward religion is never the answer. It is about a relationship between God and His people, and relationships deal with heart issues first. God is concerned about the heart of the worship that leads to a proper outward expression of love. The motivation behind the actions is the key. Outward expressions of worship that are devoid of a heart of love are never pleasing to God.

What pleases God is a worshiper, who in faith believes in Him. It is as if our hearts are turned toward God and He now is the focus of our lives. When Jesus calls for self-denial, He is asking us to place our desires, longings, passions, and lusts aside. To sum it up, He is asking us to put everything aside that we might follow Him. For some, this thought may bring a sense of apprehension and fear. If this is true for you, then honesty with God is a must. Bring your fears to Him. What God desires is for you to understand that He is always seeking the best for His children. What God wants you to understand is that laying aside all to follow Christ is, in the end, like laying aside trash for treasure. He is the treasure of all treasures.

QUESTIONS FOR REFLECTION:

- If you were to yield to Jesus and his work throughout this day, what would you feel like when it was over?
- How would your relationships be different?
- Are there any desires that "self" is demanding? Are you having trouble laying them down and yielding to Jesus? If so, be honest with God and ask Him to release you.

CHALLENGE:

Contemplate what it would mean to yield to Jesus today. If it is night, think about your day tomorrow. Think through every hour of the day. What would it look like to yield to Jesus each moment?

CHAPTER 7

Focus

Therefore we also, since we are surrounded by so great a cloud of witnesses, let us lay aside every weight, and the sin which so easily ensnares us, and let us run with endurance the race that is set before us, looking unto Jesus, the author and finisher of our faith, who for the joy that was set before Him endured the cross, despising the shame, and has sat down at the right hand of the throne of God.

Hebrews 12:1-4

THERE IS A PROGRESSION IN FOLLOWING JESUS. First, there must be desire. Secondly, there must be self-denial. Without self-denial the believer will never take up his cross. If there is never a taking up of your cross, you can never fully follow Jesus.

The eleventh chapter of Hebrews is filled with examples of men and women who lived by faith. They were all mere mortals who struggled through life like anyone else. The one thing that made them different was that they lived by faith in God. That may sound like a lot of church talk, but be assured it is not.

Simply stated, these who lived by faith knew in their hearts that God is the rewarder of those who diligently seek Him. Their trust in God led them into difficult places. This chapter teaches that there are those who do great things by faith in God, and there are some who give their life by faith in God. The common thread through all their different lives is faith.

Do you trust God to lead you to do great things in His name? Do you trust God to take you to places of pain and maybe even death? Are you willing to walk by faith in the precious Lord who loved you and gave Himself for you?

Those men and women from chapter 11 looked forward to the fulfillment of their faith. They looked ahead and died in faith waiting for that promised salvation. Jesus is their salvation and now we look back to Him as common partakers of the same faith. There salvation is our salvation. How glorious it is to see the lives of men and women who died long ago live on by their testimony of faith. Now they stand as an encouragement to those who would live by faith in this day.

They are a great cloud of witnesses and they surround us. Therefore, Let us pursue God and run the race He has set out for us. This is the encouragement at the beginning of Hebrews chapter 12 and it is an encouragement to run our race with endurance.

Preparation

Some preparation is needed before one takes off running the race. As a young man I ran track in high school. What began as break from basketball soon turned into a passion. However, it did not start out so gloriously.

For the most part, track was an individual sport and that was a change for me. It also had some unexpected surprises. For example, the uniform given to me was interesting. The shorts were a super lightweight mesh and the shirt was absurdly thin. The shoes were even more interesting. They were a mesh material with a low profile and cleats on the ball of the foot.

We began practice in long pants because of the cool, early spring weather. For a couple of weeks we practiced in warmer clothes, working on technique and form. Then, one sunny day we showed up to practice and there were boxes stacked up. Our uniforms and shoes had arrived. We excitedly picked through the boxes and went to the locker room. The first time I put the uniform on I felt uncomfortable. The clothes were so light that I felt strangely underdressed.

The shoes were uncomfortable. I was uncomfortable in the clothes, and to beat it all, I had just been named the co-captain of the track team. I had to represent. So with all the bravado I could muster up, I held my chin high and walked out of the locker room. . . completely faking it! We all got out to the track and started warming up.

Instantly, I could tell the difference in these new clothes. They were light and they moved for a runner. However, the same could not be said for the cleats. They were tight and hard to walk in. . . until the first time I ran in them.

I remember taking a jog to warm up, high-stepping to loosen up with my feet already hurting a bit. The time came for me to get in the blocks and work on the start. I got on my knees and backed into the blocks. As soon as my foot set on the block I could feel something different. The cleat gave me a stable foundation on the block. The shoes bent right behind the balls of my feet, comfortably and with ease. I got in position, made the first jump, and took about five steps toward the first hurdle when it all became clear.

The tight discomfort was crucial to keep the cleat from

moving on my foot. The traction on the front of the cleat was for running on the balls and toes of your feet. And the flexibility at the middle of the foot was to allow my foot to move in the natural running position with ease. The outfit made me free to run the race for which I was training.

In the same way, the writer of Hebrews tells the Christian to run the race in which they have been placed. In fact, we are surrounded by the testimony of those who have gone on before us and lived out their faith. They have run their race, and now we are encouraged to run ours as well. But we need to do a couple of things so we can run.

Lay Aside Every Weight

In order to run with the greatest endurance, we need to lay aside the heaviness that would keep us from running. Just as I laid aside the old heavy clothes, we are to lay aside every weight. When I ran I left my bag in the locker room, and with it I left the old heavy clothes. With those aside I was free to run.

What became obvious in the end was not obvious at the beginning. I had to learn to see things from a different perspective so that I might run my race. I had to mature as a runner and athlete. As a Christian that is the essence of sanctification. We start running the race that Christ has laid out before us. As we do this God reveals particular things in our lives that will slow us down.

If we are to learn to run, then humility and a teachable spirit are required. Agreeing with God is the only proper answer for the one who has been forgiven and freed by the grace and mercy of God. Anything else is simply rebellion. Let God have His way at this moment and let Him teach you to run with every bit of your God-given, Holy Spirit empowered strength. The discipline of being a follower of

Jesus Christ is for your good and for His glory.

What is getting in your way and keeping you from running the race that God has placed in front of you? What weight do you need to shed so that you can run free? God may well be opening your eyes to see things from a different perspective. This is the revelation of truth in your life, which allows you to see from God's perspective. What a beautiful gift of God's grace that He gives to us as we seek to follow Him. Yes, He gives us strength to live, but He also shows us the way in which we should go. As you run your race, understand that it is His Spirit who guides us unto all truth and His Word that is a guide unto our feet and a light unto our path that encourages us onward.

As we seek to deny ourselves, there is the immediate confrontation with the things in our lives that would slow us down or get in the way of our pursuit of Jesus Christ. What is it that slows you down and gets in your way when it comes to following Jesus?

One of the heaviest weights that slow the Christian down is entertainment. The desire to be entertained is inherently self-gratifying. J.C. Ryle went so far as to say, "Entertainment is man's invention to waste time." Looking to find fulfillment, we often look in unwise places.

Instead of looking to God, and denying self, we give in to the desire of sinful selfishness. We choose death while Jesus calls out to us to pursue life. Never forget that Jesus is the way, the truth, and the life. To pursue Him is to pursue life, and to pursue self is to pursue death. How much of our time is wasted in silly and menial pursuits that are unfulfilling time wasters?

Take television for example. You come in from a long day and you are tired. The first thing you might do is sit down and turn on the television. Three hours later you finally get up to go to bed.

First question: Are you rested by your three-hour entertainment sabbatical?

Second question: Are you encouraged in your faith and stronger in your pursuit of Jesus Christ?

Third question: Can you honestly say that you have been a good steward of those last three hours of your life.

We often pursue the idea of being satisfied and getting rest when what we are really looking for is renewal. "Rest" means to be reenergized, but "renewal" means to be made new. Worldly entertainment can never renew you. Only the Spirit of God can renew. So the question becomes "how do we live in light of that truth?" Entertainment takes so much of our time and often pulls us so far away.

The draw is all around us. And it's within us too. *Each one of us is tempted when we are drawn away by our own desires and enticed.* If you ever wondered how sin works, here it is. James 1 reveals, "When desire is conceived it gives birth to sin." Our own sinful desire meets up with opportunity, and when they come together sin is conceived.

Yet, in those moments if we are still and quiet, we can hear the Spirit of God and feel His call drawing us. God yearns jealously for us. When we stop quenching the Spirit and fighting against His work, then we are drawn toward this relationship with God that renews us. More than rest is to be found. Peace, joy, and comfort are found in our communion with God. It is not dependent upon outward circumstances, but rather a beautiful relationship with God where the Creator holds people in a restored relationship.

I have found that there is rarely any refreshment found in television. In our search for relaxation and rest we turn on the television and come under the hypnotic effect of visual entertainment. The senses become dulled and the brain switches to a passive mode.

Research over the last 60 years has shown rather conclusively that the brain moves from a critical thinking mode to a passive receptive one within a minute or two of watching television. When the brain begins operating in this manner it produces endorphins, which have an opiate effect on the body. So the question becomes, "Can watching television become addictive?"

An experiment in the 1970s took over 180 West Germans and offered to pay them if they could stop watching TV for one year. None resisted longer than six months and everyone said that they had become depressed and irritable during their hiatus from television.

Here is what I have found in discipleship. For the first two months of our four-month intensive discipleship program, there is no television or internet, only checking email messages for work or school. Around the third week, the entire group of students being discipled becomes extremely irritable and argumentative. Each week there are questions about loopholes and "what if's" and they seem to escalate through the first month until it comes to a head. The first time this happened it caught me off guard. Thankfully, my wife happened to be at that 6 a.m. meeting when the group started complaining and becoming a bit argumentative.

It was at this point I felt the need to be direct with the group. For the next ten minutes I spoke rather forcefully about self, pride, and arrogance and tried to help them understand what was happening in their hearts. The entire group left mad that morning. I was left scratching my head a bit, at least until the next meeting.

The next early morning meeting rolled around and the students filed in quietly; confession time began. I was amazed to see what God was doing and how He had been working in each one of their lives as they prayed and dealt with the things that God was showing them.

We all were amazed to see that God had used their desire for entertainment to expose the real heart of the issue. Pride and self-satisfaction had been their motto and now God had revealed it. They were astonished to see how much their lives had been molded by selfish desire. We are all shocked to see ourselves in light of God's holiness. When our eyes are opened to our own pull toward depravity, it is often more than we can bear. We begin to relate to Isaiah when he was confronted with the presence of God and cries out, "Woe is me for I am undone. Because I am a man of unclean lips, and I dwell in the midst of a people of unclean lips; for my eyes have seen the King, The LORD of hosts." [21]

Added to that, we live in a culture that is overly sensual. Sexual sin is rampant in our world. . . and in our churches. The statistics are staggering when it comes to how many struggle in this area. I once attended a breakfast for Christian leaders. One counselor stood up and began to talk about this topic. He said the numbers were so staggering that he had to change the questions he uses when he counsels. It is no longer a question of "Are you struggling with sexual sin?" Instead, the question has now become, "How are you dealing with the struggle of sexual sin?" Sexual sin is so rampant among the church that it has become an epidemic.

A lot of this has to do with the accessibility of entertainment. You can now get all forms of entertainment on your computer and phone, as well as the television. There used to be a time when you had to look for pornographic material. Now, you have to be careful to not let it land in your inbox.

If you were to be honest with yourself, it would be hard to say that those hours of your life in pursuit of entertainment were spent well. How many marriages and families would be strengthened and maybe even saved if communication and fellowship took the place of endless hours of mind numbing entertainment? Our desire for entertainment is nothing less than a sinful addiction, which has its core in selfish satisfaction.

While the easy accessibility to entertainment is at best a distraction, this is only a symptom of the real issue. The problem is pride that desires sinful self-satisfaction. Pride whispers sensually into the ear of us all, trying to convince us that "we deserve this" or "it is our right to have this for ourselves." Instead of self-denial leading to life, we choose self-gratification, leading to death.

The whole point is to lay aside every weight. There is no doubt that there are things that slow us down and hinder us from living the Christian life. The enemy is constantly trying to offer us things to try on or to put in our pockets, that we might be heavy laden with the cares of this world. They are needless distractions of a fallen world.

What is slowing you down in your pursuit of Jesus Christ? Could it be that you have the wrong goals in life? Have you set yourself on a course that is man-centered with its selfish ambitions and desires? If so, you are not the only one in history to do so.

The Apostle Paul had set himself on a path to grab all that he could in life. He said that he was "circumcised the eighth day, of the stock of Israel, of the tribe of Benjamin, a Hebrew of the Hebrews; concerning the law, a Pharisee; concerning zeal, persecuting the church; concerning the righteousness which is in the law, blameless."

If there were ever a go-getter in the Bible, it would be the Apostle Paul. Most people need to be prompted to do something, but Paul had to be slowed down. His heritage was of the Hebrew nation and he could trace it back all the way through his particular tribe of Benjamin. Paul had the pedigree. He had the drive. He had the fame and power. He was the Hebrew poster child. His whole life revolved around his heritage, and he was proud of it. This led him to be zealous and hard-charging to the point he was willing to crush any and all that stood in the way. When it came to the law, Paul was an expert among experts. Type A and driven hard to be the best. Finally, concerning keeping the law. . . blameless. That meant no one could look into his life and pin anything on him that was unlawful. Paul was at the top of the game and getting things done. But Paul was wrong. In the same manner that Paul had lived, He would be confronted.

Abruptly, Jesus stopped Paul on the road to Damascus. Jesus knocked Paul down, blinded him, and then spoke audibly to him. Paul would ask Jesus "Who are you?" and "What do you want me to do?" Paul is then led to Damascus. Do not let what happens next go unnoticed.

And he was three days without sight and neither ate nor drank. – Acts 9:9

I believe, based upon Paul's life and writings, that he was completely and utterly broken. Everything that he had lived for and desired had now been turned upside down. Undoubtedly, it was three days of repentance, contemplation, forgiveness, and freedom. From that point on, everything changed, and he would eventually write the following words that would express the heartbeat of what it means to be a Christian: "Indeed, I count everything as loss because of the surpassing worth of knowing Christ

Jesus my Lord."

It was no longer about outward religiousness, but now it was about a relationship with Jesus Christ. The desire to know Christ was far more important than what he could gain in this life. There was no comparison between Jesus and personal gain. What are you living for these days?

Wrong Thinking/Wrong Living

There is another thing that weighs the Christian down. This gets a little closer to the heart and exposes what we practically believe. It is the way we think. There is often a difference in what we say we believe and how we live. How we live out our lives show more of what we believe than what we proclaim to believe. To think wrongly about God, circumstances, and about life will always slow us down. When we begin to think wrong, the actions that proceed from that thinking will lead us in wrong directions.

In ministering to people over the years, I have often seen wrong thinking lead to wrong actions. I have often referred to this as "stinking thinking." That may sound a bit elementary but the description is true. And the core of wrong thinking could be as simple as not knowing what is true.

Ignorance plays a big part in the weak Christian's life. We must dive the depths of God's Word. The richness of God's Word should saturate our lives. When you read the Scriptures, the Holy Spirit will show you these things and all of the sudden you are confronted by what is true, by what is right, and by what is holy. In those moments the light of Jesus Christ exposes the weakness and frailty of our humanity. We come to those places and begin to see that we desperately need God to move in our lives. We need His grace to give us what we do not have and cannot get in our own strength. We need His mercy to give us forgiveness and cleansing that we can never earn own our own. It is crucial that the Christian seek God through His Word. A Christian who does not know the Word of God and is not in the Word of God is one who will live a spiritually poor and beggarly life.

I received a phone call one afternoon from a young Christian worker who had felt called to a particularly difficult circumstance. As we began to talk, I immediately sensed that something was not right in his life. I sat there and listened to the difficulties and struggles for a few moments, and then I asked one question. "How long has it been since you have spent time with God and have been in the Word?" The quiet response was, "A couple of months."

Sadly, I explained the situation to him. Due to a distant relationship with God there was not spiritual strength. With no spiritual strength there was no battle with the flesh. Without Jesus, flesh wins. When flesh wins, wrong decisions are sure to follow. He had made some wrong decisions, and it was heart-breaking to hear the consequences of those decisions. Making sinful decisions in life is the quickest way to misery for the Christian.

What is absurd is for the follower of Christ to have the answers and never seek them out. The tendency of the flesh is to reject and push away from God, but the Spirit of God is calling the believer back. Do not reject this divine call. Surrender immediately and quit pushing against the Faithful Redeemer of our soul.

To daily set your heart and mind on the things of God is to point your life in the direction of holiness and righteous living. That is why Paul told the believers in the Philippian church to think in a certain way.

Whatever things are true, whatever things are noble,

whatever things are just, whatever things are pure, what- ever things are lovely, whatever things are of good report, if there is any virtue and if there is anything praiseworthy— meditate on these things.

The discipline of meditation is by in large lost in the Western culture. It has been relegated to the Eastern philosophies and religions. Eastern religions use medita- tion in hopes of reaching a higher plane of existence by calming the mind. However, to meditate in a Scriptural sense is to take a truth of God and fill your heart, soul, and mind with that truth. Psalm 1 demonstrates, "Delight is in the law of the Lord and on His law he meditates day and night." The one who meditates on God's Law is "like a tree planted by rivers of water that will bear its fruit in its season, whose leaf shall not wither, and whatever he does shall prosper." A simple way to sum this up is to ask the question, "Where is your focus?"

QUESTIONS FOR REFLECTION:

Entertainment is not only consuming but often spiritually and morally degrading. Let us now ask some questions of our entertainment.

- Has viewing TV for hours encouraged you to love God and others more?
- Are you drawing closer to God through this time of entertaining.
- Are you more or less holy in the way you think?
- What could or should you have been doing during those hours?

CHALLENGE:

In our intensive discipleship we disconnect from entertainment for 40 days. If you are reading this on your own, start by turning off the TV and staying off your computer for one solid week. Only get online to check email and then immediately get off the computer. The struggle may be intense but the change will be dramatic. Fill any free time focusing on your relationship with God and with others.

CHAPTER 8

Tangled

JUST AS THERE ARE THINGS THAT SLOW US DOWN, there are other things that are clearly sinful. To both of these, the writer of Hebrews says to lay them aside. When it comes to sin, the writer of Hebrews qualifies the sin by saying, "the sin which so easily ensnares us." There is a clear warning from God to be careful of those things that could easily trip us up. In other words, as you walk through life be careful where you step. This fallen world is full of potholes, trip wires, and debris that have been scattered around to cause believers to stumble.

When I was 9 years old my family moved to the mountains. It was a breath of fresh air for us kids. We lived in an old farmhouse surrounded by cow pastures and mountains. One spring day we were out behind the house, past the pasture at the tree line with a friend of ours. My brother went around a big oak tree and all of the sudden the biggest bird I had ever seen flew up in the tree. It was a wild turkey. I looked up, startled at the sight and sound. I was mesmerized. What I didn't know is that my little brother had ran around that big oak. His yell of amazement jerked me back into reality. I looked back down toward the bottom of the tree and little grey chicks scattered from behind the tree with my grinning brother chasing them down. That is when craziness began.

I was standing there in amazement, our friend was laughing and my brother was running in circles chasing a bunch of little turkeys when something caught my eye. I glanced up to see an enormous turkey coming straight for us. We immediately turned to run through the field back to the house. This particular field was a hay field. There were no cattle on it in order for the grass to grow tall for hay, so naturally it was thick and hard to run through. Halfway across the field the turkey was still after us. We broke through the field and hit the fence line. Now all that stood in our way were three strands of barbed wire.

When I got to the fence I never broke stride. One foot hit the second wire and I jumped, hoping to miss the top wire. I sprung off the ground headfirst over the fence and all was going well until that one sharp barb caught my jeans. Flipping over the fence and landing on my back, I looked up just long enough to see my brother and his friend going over the top of me and headed for safety. Thankfully, the turkey finally stopped chasing us. That barbed wire fence tangled me up. I was headed for home and for safety, but in my hurried carelessness I had been tripped up and potentially could have been badly injured.

As a Christian, we must always be careful. Of course, we are headed for the safety of our heavenly home. But, as we run through life we must be careful. There are things lying all around that can trip us up and tangle us on our journey. There may even be some things that have the propensity to trip you up in your life right now. One barb stopped me and put me on my back. Be careful in life and walk with the understanding because the spiritual danger could only be one step away.

Pay Attention

I love old movies where the soldiers are walking through the jungle and one young soldier makes a careless move. Suddenly, he steps to close to a trip wire, and an older more experienced soldier stops him just short of death, teaching the young one a valuable and life-saving lesson. That lesson is to pay attention.

It is not only a crucial lesson for the soldier, but it is likewise a lesson for the believer. The Apostle Paul says, "Pay careful attention, then, to how you walk—not as unwise people but as wise making the most of the time."[22] In the original language the idea is one of accuracy. Therefore, the thought is to "watch carefully that you walk accurately." When the New Testament uses the word "walk" it is describing the manner in which one lives. So pay attention to the manner in which you live.

Carelessly walking through life is dangerous. If you walk with God and live according to His purposes, it will be no accident. The soldier carefully measures his steps along the trail, so too must the Christian consider his steps along the path of life. There is no overestimating the importance of walking with God step by step.

It is important to understand that as we follow Jesus we will actually emulate His life. If we say we know Him and abide in Him, ought we not walk in the same way He walked? [23] There are a number of ways the Word of God describes what it means to walk with God.

One is the concept of light. In the beginning, God spoke and said, "Let there be light." And there was light. On the command of the Creative Word there came a separation of light and dark. What darkness once covered, now light exposed. What a beautiful foreshadowing of what would happen in a fallen world. The Creator of light would enter back into His creation once again, bringing light into a dark and fallen world. He *is* the Light of the World.

Salvation would come through His sacrifice and life would come by His resurrection. Therefore, the Light of the World, Jesus, would shine His light into the hearts of people exposing that darkness.

When one turns to God in faith and receives the forgiveness and salvation of Jesus Christ, he becomes a bearer of that light. The light that exposed and changed him is now part of who he has become. Jesus would make this point when He would say to His disciples, "You are the light of the world."[24]

Therefore, the logical outcome of the life that has been transformed by the light of the gospel is to now shine that light as we live in the world.

This is where the beauty and simplicity of the Christian life become so evident. We simply live according to the light of Jesus Christ. We find the answer to living out this Christian life in fullness and walking the victory over sin that Jesus Christ secured is as simple as walking in his light.

Humanity often tries to make things so difficult when, at the core, there is such simplicity in the message and in the manner of salvation that a child can understand it. Yet the work of salvation is so deep and rich that a lifetime of contemplation will only touch the surface of the grandeur of what our God has done.

In the end, the Christian life is simple. Understand that the nature of humanity is corrupt with sin. The penalty on humanity was pronounced. The wages of sin is death. There was a true and literal death of man's relationship with God. Judgment is pronounced on all who sin and all have sinned. . . but One! That is why the cross can be all at once so beautiful and yet so horrible. Its beauty is that it was the place where the sinless Son of God willingly laid down His life. However, what makes the cross so horrible is that it was my sin that had to be taken care of on that cross. The wrath of God the Father was poured out on the Son. Now the greatest gift that humanity could ever receive is being offered. The gift of forgiveness and reconciliation is given to you. As with any gift, you choose to take it or not. By faith confess your sin, reach out and receive the gift of salvation by saying, "Yes Lord, save me, forgive me, and change me." Now go follow Him.

Now we have spiritual life in Christ and it is leading to eternal life. The believer's physical death is not one of sorrow, but joy and hope, understanding that the death is the veil that must be passed through, leading to the presence of God and eternal life. This is complete salvation.

Reminiscent of Genesis 1, John writes, "In Him was life, and the life was the light of men. And the light shines in the darkness, and the darkness did not comprehend it."[25] The basic fact of the Christian life is that we are a new creation in Jesus Christ. Our spiritually dead person has been crucified and we are dead to self. The word "different" does not even begin to describe what this new person has become. The biblical word for this is "holy," which means to be "set apart." In Jesus we are holy as He is holy. We are alive as He is alive, and we are headed to be with Him where He is! This is the wondrous truth that gives us strength and hope to live out the Christ-life in this world.

We must never stop with shedding weights and laying aside sin that can easily entangle us. No, we must run our race with eyes toward the finish line.

QUESTIONS FOR REFLECTION:

- Are you walking carefully in this world? Are there any situations or relationships that are potential snares for your life?
- Are you walking in places you should not be?
- Are you relying on God and resting in His grace to help you live moment by moment?

CHALLENGE:

Think of three people who have failed morally either in relationships, business, or politics. What were the snares and weights that led them down the wrong path? Take those things that were detrimental and see if there are any of them in your life. If there are, ask God to help you deal with them right now.

CHAPTER 9

Author and Finisher

A FOLLOWER OF JESUS CHRIST SHOULD ALWAYS seek to remove the weight and lay aside sin that would entangle. However, if we stop there, we will miss the whole point of what God is saying to us in Hebrews 12.

The writer goes on to demonstrate, "let us run the race with endurance the race that is set before us." We are to run this race of faith. We come to this place and understand that before Christ, we were heckling spectators in the great assembly of sinners. We were rejecting God and being a part of dissident humanity, seeking its own way.

God comes into the stands and invites us to come join in the race, but before this can happen you must be qualified to run in the race.

In order to make the Olympics, in many countries there are a number of trials or races that have to be run. In those races you have to finish close to the front in order to qualify. That is one aspect of qualification.

The other equally important qualification is that you must be a citizen of the country, which, you intend to represent. Performance and citizenship are the keys to being qualified to run the race.

Jesus takes us out of the stands and qualifies us. The cross of Jesus Christ is the place where He finished the qualifier on our account and has now offered that to us.

So when someone puts their faith in Jesus Christ, the righteousness of Jesus Christ is placed on that person, covering them and qualifying that one for the race.

The other aspect of being qualified is that in Christ we are no longer strangers and foreigners, but fellow citizens with the saints and members of the household of God.[26] In these two ways the Christians have been qualified to run the race that God has set before us.

Jesus takes us out of the stands, qualifies us, and sets us in our lane. At salvation our race begins. It is not just any race. It is a race of endurance. What is interesting about Hebrews 12 is what is not said. There is no talk of competition between runners. The race is not against other Christians as competitors. The race is against time.

Each one of us has been given days on this earth, and those days will come to an end. Our life on this earth is like a vapor, it will be here one day and over the next. It is imperative to grasp the idea that there is a time constraint on our race. There is a goal and that is to run our race well and have an enduringly strong finish.

Endurance means to have strength over the long-term. The race of faith requires endurance and this endurance does not happen in our own strength. The power of the Holy Spirit strengthens us to run the race in which God has placed us. We do that by trusting in the Holy Spirit and by leaning on Him as we run. We need not thirst because He is the Living Water. We need not grow weary with hunger, for He is the Bread of Life. We need not tire with a loss of breath, for He is the Breath of Life. All that we need He has provided.

Having shed the weights and entanglements of this world and denying sinful self, the follower of Jesus is now free to run the supernaturally empowered race of faith. It is important to keep the entire race in mind. Run with wisdom so that you might run with endurance and remember that without a finish line a race becomes just another run.

When we think of a race, we inherently think of the finish line. One day this life will soon be past. Scripture tells us to redeem the time because the days are evil. That means that these days we live in are evil and we are to take them back by the payment of Holy Spirit empowered self-denial.

The Apostle Paul writes, "But I discipline my body and bring it into subjection, lest, when I have preached to others, I myself should become disqualified." [27] The good grace of God strengthens us and frees us from the power of sin and death but our flesh is fallen and corrupt. It fights against the things of the Spirit. When we yield to the Spirit of God, obedience will follow.

No one is saying that the race will not be difficult and painful at times. But the good news is that no matter how difficult the race may be, you have the power and the person of God at work in you to help you as you run.

Let's face it, we all get weary. It is a long race. But, God through his Spirit strengthens, comforts and helps us to run. In the 1992 Olympics in Barcelona, the world watched as British 400 meter runner Derek Redmond took the starting blocks. He had already had the fastest time in round 1 and had went on to place first in his quarterfinal.

The starting gun went off and the field was close around the back stretch when something went wrong. Derek grabbed the back of his right leg and slowed to a hop. His hamstring had snapped rendering the leg nearly useless. That is when something amazing happened.

He would not stop, he would not accept a stretcher,

and he would not quit. He hobbled around the track as the runners looked back from beyond the finish line and the crowd got strangely quiet. That is when they realized he would not quit. He would endure the pain. It looked like he would not make it as the pain increased. From the sideline, a figure, pushing past security and officials ran onto the track. It was Derek Redmond's father. He ran up to his son and put his arm around him to lift him up. As Derek realized it was his father, he broke down in sobs and leaned into his father as the heartbreak of all those years of work ended in a torn hamstring. As others tried to help, the father swatted their hands away. He would finish with his son.

It became one of the most inspiring sports stories of all time. In the same way, we have a Father who loves and cares for us as we run our race. There may be those days you need the Father to help you finish that race and when you do, you can lean on Him. He will accept your sobs of pain and heartbreak. He will give you strength to finish and walk you to the finish line.

Here is the exciting part! Jesus stands just past the finish line with His arms open wide. There, the Savior stands ready to receive the weary runner. The view of Him will encourage the weariest of souls and will be a reminder of how the lover of our souls bids us come.

Therefore, we are to look to Jesus, the author and finisher of our faith! In the end our focus is on Jesus Christ. Now go back for a moment and consider the illustration.

Lanes

When we enter our race God sets us in a specific lane. The lines are there for a reason, and it is possible to come out of our lane. On a track the lines serve two purposes.

One is to guide you down the track in your lane. The other is to keep you out of someone else's lane. Within those two lines you are free to run your race. You have room to move your arms and legs as you wish.

However, when you cross over the lines something is wrong. If you do not keep your eyes focused on the finish it actually becomes easy to stray from your lane. One wrong step can send you veering off, and it is easy to do if you are looking down at your feet. Likewise, if you look up into the stands or look across the track lanes your body will tend to follow your head. As a runner in the race of faith, it is easy to focus on yourself and misstep. If you are focused on the things of this world, it is easy to head off in the direction of those things. Only by keeping your focus on Jesus and your finish line will you run the straight course.

As a senior in high school I ran the anchor leg of the 4x100 relay. I was the last guy to receive the baton coming around turn and heading down the home stretch to the finish. There is a certain zone in which the teammate coming up can hand off to the teammate in front, so the timing must be precise.

At one particular track meet we were running the race, and as my teammate was getting close I began to run. At this point we had a sizeable lead. I began to gain speed as the runner closed in on me. I reached back with palm up and the baton swept down into my hand. That is when everything went into slow motion. I pulled my right hand forward to move into the sprint position and somehow the baton had not landed firmly in my hand. As my hand moved up, the baton went flying out of my hand across three lanes and landed with a bounce.

Stunned, I had to wait for everyone to pass by because if I strayed out of my lane and impeded the progress of another runner, then my whole team would be disqualified. I found myself going from first to fourth place in a second. I grabbed the baton, got refocused on the finish line, and with a lot of adrenaline, caught back up to second place.

My mistake had cost our whole team. I was devastated. How much more devastating is it for the Christian to run the race of faith not living up to his or her God given potential? There must be a diligence and focus to run within the lines of God's Word. If you stray across the lines you will bring harm to yourself, to those around you, and God is dishonored. Never think that your sin only affects you. That is a lie from the father of lies. Your life is so interconnected to others that if you do not live by the power of the Spirit, it will discourage those around you.

God has set us in a race, and we are to put aside any weight and entanglement and run the race with endurance. Know that you are strengthened to run by the power of the Holy Spirit. Understand that Jesus stands waiting for you at the end of your race. May these thoughts have a purifying effect. Be encouraged that other believers are running their race all around you. Encourage them and receive encouragement as you look to the finish line. Run with your eyes on Jesus.

QUESTIONS FOR REFLECTION:

- What does it mean for you and other believers when the Bible reveals you are a citizen with the saints and members of the household of God?
- One day when your life is over and your race is run, what will you want to have accomplished? What are you pursuing in this life?
- How are you representing the household of God in this world?

CHALLENGE:

Think about the end. When this life is over what will you want your family and friends to have said about you? If your life were to end today, what would God say about your life to this point? Think about it and write the answers to these questions down. They will have a clarifying effect on your life.

Chapter 10

Nevertheless

He went a little farther and fell on His face, and prayed, saying, "O My Father, if it is possible, let this cup pass from Me; nevertheless, not as I will, but as You will." Then He came to the disciples and found them sleeping, and said to Peter, "What! Could you not watch with Me one hour? Watch and pray, lest you enter into temptation. The spirit indeed is willing, but the flesh is weak." Again, a second time, He went away and prayed, saying, "O My Father, if this cup cannot pass away from Me unless I drink it, Your will be done."

Matthew 26:39-42

UNDERSTANDING DEEP SPIRITUAL TRUTHS MAY be difficult at times. Any good teacher will illustrate points with stories to explain what is being taught. Illustrations are the colors between the lines of the painting that give it clarity, and often the strongest illustrations are those that deal with real life. The Bible is full of those life stories that God meant for us to understand so that we might learn who He is, who we are, what went wrong with humanity. Above all, God wants us to know how, through Jesus Christ, He is making it right.

You don't have to look far for clarity. Jesus illustrates perfect self-denial. The Lord of lords and the King of kings not only illustrates it, but also demonstrates to us what this looks like when He humbles Himself in the Garden of Gethsemane. There is no doubt that this is the ultimate illustration concerning self-denial. It is a picture devoid of sin and yet in its essence, human. Therefore, the illustration is as perfect as the One illustrating it. Any other sacrifice that we might see in history alludes to that perfect sacrifice of Jesus Christ.

As a background to this passage, Jesus had already spoken of His death, burial, and resurrection a number of times. Jesus would make it so clear that He would say, "The Son of Man must suffer many things, and be rejected by the elders and chief priests and scribes, and be killed, and after three days rise again."

Jesus has come to this point in His life and ministry and He is now at the crossroads. He comes to the garden, which bears the name Gethsemane.[28] The name of the garden is significant because the name means, "oil press." It was a place where there was an actual olive press with a large stone that would crush the olives in order that they would give up their precious oil.

My wife and I had the opportunity to go the Middle East some years ago. During our time there we visited a working olive grove and press. It was a historical site that used an animal to turn the press. It was amazing to see. There was round stone that sat upright and it weighed hundreds of pounds. It rolled in a circle over another flat stone. The olives would be crushed by the monstrous wheel, thus releasing the oil to run down grooves into a catch basin. Jesus was in one of these gardens. Olive oil was important in the life of Israel in a number of ways. For example,

God had commanded that the children of Israel bring pure oil of pressed olives for the light, to cause the lamp to burn continually in the tabernacle of meeting.[29] What a beautiful picture. Foreshadowing He who would be the Light of the world. Jesus would be pressed in the garden. What is inside the olive flows under the weight of the press. Likewise, that which was in the heart of Jesus would come out under the pressure of God's will. On that night, love leading to obedience in the heart of Jesus flowed.

Under the intense pressure of that evening, Jesus prayed three times; if there was any other way, let this cup pass from Him. The cup was, in a sense, everything that would happen in the next 24 hours. It included being deserted by those He loved, beaten, ridiculed, and ending in death on the cross. Jesus would take the place of the sinner by having the sin of humanity placed upon Him, thus accepting the full wrath of God.

He knew what had been revealed as He prayed in the Garden. With that knowledge He comes to the Father and asks if there is any other way for this cup to pass from him. This human, yet sinless question is startlingly uttered from the Son of God. This expression of humanity is absolutely true and honest. Our identification with Jesus in this moment becomes personal. For, who would not request another way? Surely, if Jesus would ask this of the Father, then would we not find ourselves asking the same question? In His humanity He asks according to His own will. But with the question comes a caveat.

Jesus asks for another way, but before He is finished speaks one important word, "nevertheless."[30] The weight of this word can hardly be overstated. The root word means, "Something is greater or more excellent." It represents the doorway to the abundant and God-honoring Christian life.

Go Disciple

However, before abundant life comes absolute surrender. "Nevertheless" recognizes that I as an individual have a will and desire a specific way. For the sake of the argument, let us not even delineate whether the desire is sinful or not. Let us just say that the individual has a will. "Nevertheless" says, "Yes, I have a will, but I desire God's will above my own." This is the heart of worship expressed in a word. When Jesus came to the Garden of the olive press, He asked for a different way with humility and submission desiring that God the Father have His will in the life and actions of the Son.

This is the picture of what it looks like to deny self. It is to lay aside our own desires, wants, and needs for the will of God. This sounds like a bad deal if you look at from a human perspective. However, if in your mind and heart you have begun to understand the greatness of God and the majestic purpose for which He has created you, then you can start to see the eternal reward of obedience. The blessing of God's way over your own yields fruitfulness in this life and an eternal reward to come.

"Nevertheless" then becomes the doorway to continuing on in the will of God. Without this response to our own will and life, we will never go on to take up our cross. We look unto Jesus, the Author and Finisher of our faith. He asks us to come and follow Him on this journey of eternal life. The Great Shepherd leads us into blessing, and part of that blessing is being free from ourselves.

Hebrews 12:2 further describes Jesus by revealing, "He is the author and finisher of our faith. . . for the joy that was set before Him endured the cross, despising the shame, and has sat down at the right hand of the throne of God."

The Originator who matures our faith endured the cross for the joy that was set before Him. It may seem paradoxical to speak of joy when talking about the cross. Jesus knew that He would have to suffer and become the thing that He despised. . . our sin. So where is the joy in that situation?

The joy of Jesus comes first in that He accomplished what the Father had sent Him to do. It is amazing to consider that Jesus finished without failure. I would be happy with getting through a day without some type of failure! He lived in perfect obedience for 33 years, finishing what God had called Him to do.

What an encouragement for the Christian to know that Jesus is our High Priest who can sympathize with our weakness because He was tempted in all points as we are and yet without sin. Therefore, we can boldly come to the throne of grace, that we may obtain mercy and find grace to help in a time of need because at that throne we find Jesus Christ Himself seated at the right hand. When we come in that moment to find and obtain mercy and grace, God, in His perfect justice, looks to Jesus and in the throne room of Heaven, forgiveness is pronounced on the guilty because Jesus has paid the price. This sacrifice leads me to humble thankfulness and worship of God. That is the joy that was set before Jesus Christ. It was about obedience to the Father.

Second, the joy that was set before Him involves the salvation of humanity. Jesus was our only hope. And out of the depths of His eternal love for the Father and for others, He willingly went to the cross and secured salvation for all those who would believe.

In the end, the complete self-denial of Jesus led to obedience and to fulfilling the will of the Father. When Christians comes to a place of self-denial, they come into obedience and move onto the narrow path of fulfilling the will of God. We identify with Jesus. This is of great importance in the Christian life. God knows the story. God has the plan. Therefore, it is only logical that we should yield to the wisdom of God, for He alone sees all the outcomes and consequences to our actions.

In the first garden man sinned. The disobedience of Adam caused immediate spiritual death, and it lead to the physical death of man. In the second Garden Jesus obeyed, and it gave way to spiritual life and is leading to eternal life. What rebellious people lost in the first garden, the obedient Jesus secured in the second garden. May you enter into the Garden of Obedience, where you are sure to find the grace of God. And remember, what you are giving up does not compare to what He is offering.

QUESTIONS FOR REFLECTION:

- Have you come to the place of "nevertheless" in your life?
- Are you completely surrendered to the will of God? If not, what is standing in the way?
- Will you be able to find joy and peace that surpasses all understanding anywhere else?
- The Lord is working in your life. Are you agreeing with Him and His work?

CHALLENGE:

Begin using the word "nevertheless" as part of your regular vocabulary. When what you want to do comes into conflict with what you should do, say, "Nevertheless, not my will, but your will be done" as you yield to the Lord.

CHAPTER 11

Take Up Your Cross

COMING TO THE PLACE WHERE YOU CAN HON-
estly say "nevertheless" is the doorway to the sacrificial life. Jesus exemplified that and fully accepted the way
God the Father had shown Him. He rose up from prayer in
the garden with the path of the Father clearly before Him,
and that path would lead Him to the cross.

When you hear the word "cross" a number of things
may come to mind. You may think of a gold ornament
worn around the neck, that thing on top of the steeple on a
church building, or you may even think of a ghastly scene
with Jesus hanging between heaven and earth. Whatever
your thoughts may be, the cross is the central symbol of
Christianity and for good reason.

It is the place where the sinless Son of God would die
for the sins of humanity. He was spiritually right in every
way. This led to a perfect morality, which in turn proved
that this One had *no* penalty to pay. This is the only way He
who knew no sin could become sin for us and give those
who would, by faith, believe on His perfect righteousness.
Our lack of holiness had separated us from God. The sin
had now been dealt with, allowing for the restoration of a
relationship with our Creator.

I love discussing these truths in small groups. It usually
begins the same way. At first, there are the surface answers

and I usually let those play out for a few moments. Then I begin to probe deeper. I have often asked the question, "What are some words that describe the cross?" The answers that usually come out are obedience, salvation, humility, and submission. But the answer that I look for in those discussions is particular. It is the word *sac*rifice. The cross was a place of sacrifice, first and foremost.

The writer of Hebrews demonstrates, "But now, once at the end of the ages, He has appeared to put away sin by the sacrifice of Himself."[31] The Old Testament sacrificial system was a continual process of bringing a sacrifice, placing it on the altar, and offering it up to God. The sacrifice was brought to the altar in faith and hope that God would accept the offering and make atonement for sin. The only problem with this is that the priest who received the offering had to make an offering for himself and his family as well. So year after year the families would come and offer a sacrifice for their sin.

Jesus was different. While every priest would stand ministering daily and offering repeatedly the same sacrifices, which could never take away sins. . . this Man, after He had offered one sacrifice for sins forever, sat down at the right hand of God, from that time waiting till His enemies are made His footstool. [32] All of the Old Testament sacrifices were pointing to the time when the ultimate sacrifice would take place. They were foreshadows of the reality that was to come with the sacrifice of the Messiah.

Jesus offered Himself as the perfect sacrifice. Perfect, in a biblical sense, means complete, and His salvation is most definitely complete. The application of that truth for the believer means that all of our sin is forgiven if we have, by faith, come to Him, in repentance, asking for forgiveness. Consider that every sin you have ever committed has been covered by the precious blood of Jesus. His sacrifice is perfectly complete.

What does this mean for the believer? It means freedom. Your guilt and shame has been dealt with by the work of Jesus. You can now live free from the eternal and damning penalty of sin. Do you understand this truth? Are you living in the bondage of the past? If so, let God remind you of His truth and work, contemplating His forgiveness. Live with joy!

At salvation a person is uniquely united with Jesus Christ. This uniting is spiritual in nature. We often think about our physical surroundings as being reality, but this physical world we live in is a product of the spiritual world. Never forget that this world was created by God who is Spirit, and those who worship Him must worship in spirit and truth.[33] Therefore, we must think spiritually when it comes to life. This life is not to be lived according to a set of outward standards alone, but in communion with our Creator. At salvation there is a unity that occurs which is real and unmistakable. The reason for this is because what we once were has now been recreated with the pure, undeniable holiness of God.

Paul gives a wonderful word on this in Romans 6. The passage speaks to the spiritual reality of those who have a relationship with Jesus Christ. We have been united together in the likeness of His death. The old man, as Scripture calls him, is our sinful spiritual self who is dead in sin and can never desire the things of God. When that old person is unified with Christ and His work on the cross, the old person is dealt with spiritually and now unified in the perfect death.

Therefore, those who know Him can confidently say that I am crucified with Christ, it is no longer I who live but Christ lives within me, and the life which I live in this (body) flesh I now live by faith in the Son of God who gave Himself for me. [34] What joy and peace fills the heart of the one who has experienced this union with the Lord. For if we have been united together in the likeness of His death, certainly we also shall be in the likeness of His resurrection. This means that before there can ever be the hope of new life, the old cursed and sinful life must be dealt with permanently. Our old man was crucified with Him.

How sad it is for the Christian to walk around like a spiritual beggar when you have been made a son or daughter. As children of God, the cross of Jesus Christ covered the penalty of sin past, present, and future. If that is so, then the question to follow is, "Why do I have to take up my cross?" In order to grasp the meaning of this statement we need to understand what our cross is not. It is certainly not a means to earn the grace of God for our lives. His grace and salvation are a gift. If Jesus paid our sin debt on His cross, then it must mean something other than paying for sin when I am instructed to "take up my cross." Indeed it does.

Identification

I know that I am spiritually united with Jesus. What happens spiritually always leads to what happens physically. If a man or woman has been changed by the Spirit of God and reborn spiritually in the likeness of Christ, then outward change must occur. The one changed begins to live according to this fundamental spiritual change. There is an outward manifestation of the inward reality. The reality is that the Spirit of the Son has been sent into our hearts. If this is true, as Jesus walked, I am to walk. As Jesus talked, I am to talk, as He lived, I am to live.

Identification with Jesus is therefore inherent in the Christian life. The first line of identification with Jesus Christ is love and obedience. These two cannot be separate in the Christian life. Jesus was once asked, "What is the greatest command?" His response was, "You shall love the Lord your God with all your heart, with all your soul, with all your strength, and with all your mind,' and 'your neighbor as yourself."[35] What is stunning about this statement is that there is a command, which requires obedience. But to be obedient, you have to love. I am to love God and love others, and in doing so I will be obedient.

Jesus clearly exemplifies His love for the Father in the Garden. His desire is for the Father's will to be done even though it would cost Him everything. Paul reminds us in Philippians, "He became obedient to the point of death, even death on the cross."

For the believer, the first point of identification is love leading to obedience. Jesus said, "He who has My commandments and keeps them, it is he who loves Me. And he who loves Me will be loved by My Father, and I will love him and manifest Myself to him."[36] If we profess love for God, then we will confess that love to God and to the world through a life of obedience. If you want a quick spiritual checkup, begin by asking yourself the question, "Am I loving God?" If the answer is "yes" then it must also be true that you love others even as yourself.

There will be those times where the Lord confronts you and allows you to see whether you are living in this loving obedience. Those times are not always pleasant, but they are fruitful.

I once had the opportunity to listen to the president of the Gideon's International. They are the ones who hand out Bibles all over the world. It is an amazing organization.

As I listened to the president speak to the crowd about the numbers of people who do not even know the name of Jesus, I really began to question myself, my family, and my church. Were any of us really making a difference for lost humanity?

If that was not enough, one of the last pictures he showed was a group of hands reaching out toward a man. What you could barely see was that the man had only one Gideon New Testament. All of those people were grasping for the Word of God, but there was only one to give away.

The real question that stuck in my heart that day was, "Do I really love God?" There is a world out there grasping for something to believe in, and I have the answer. I have the resources. Am I just talking a good game? Because if I love God, then I will love others. And that leads to action. The one who would follow Jesus cannot sit by and watch the lost perish and sleep well at night. On the contrary, he or she will seek to love God and love others, and that will always lead to action. The action is to make disciples.

In order to love others in this way there will have to be self-denial. Unconditional love is costly and does not seek its own. What is your heart seeking? Is it to love God with all that you are and all that you have or is it to love yourself and make your own decisions living life on your terms? How is it in your love for others? Are you seeking the good of others or are you envious of what others have in relationships, talents, or position? If so, understand that the root cause of sin itself is pride. Pride always demands for *self*. As Jesus took up His cross and his responsibility in fulfilling the will of God, we identify and exemplify the Lord by taking up our cross.

That leads to another aspect of identification with Jesus Christ: Humility. Humility is simply a lowering of self before others. Humility never demands its own way, even if wrong is being done to you for no reason. That may make you uncomfortable. However, you will find it to be true.

How Far Do You Go in Humility?

The apostle Peter wrote a practical chapter on Christian living in the letter of I Peter. In chapter two, he speaks to a number of issues, including submission to the governing authorities, particularly the emperor of the time. Peter then transitions into teaching on servants submitting to earthly masters.

He begins by telling servants to be submissive not only to the good and gentle, but also to the harsh. Then he makes a startling statement: "For this is commendable, if because of conscience toward God one endures grief, suffering wrongly." That sounds terribly unfair and the worst part, or so it seems, is that it is commendable before God! Before you jump to conclusions, listen to why Peter says it.

He explains that there is no honor in suffering when you deserve it. However, if you suffer when you do not deserve it and you suffer because of your *good conscience toward God,* you actually fall in line with the Jesus Christ Himself and as Peter says, "For to this you were called, because Christ also suffered for us, leaving us an example, that you should follow His steps."

Peter takes Christian living to the extreme by explaining how far we are to go to live and be like Jesus. The simple answer is *all the way*. If you can come to this understanding, then life becomes beautifully simple.

A few years ago, I led a team of students on a trip to tell people about Jesus. I was working with a specific tribe in a land and culture that was so different than my own. I was amazed as I began to learn about the people and their religion. The men of this culture were known for being fierce warriors. These were hard chargers, and they went into battle with seemingly little fear. This tribe's lack of fear led those they fought to be wary and fearful in battle. As I began to discuss this trait among some of their people, I quickly understood where the lack of fear in battle came from, and I was stunned.

These people believed that when they died in battle that they would instantly be reborn into a family in their people group. Therefore, when they went into battle there was no reason to let fear overtake them. Their belief system, as wrong as it was, taught them that they had nothing to fear. So they were willing to go all the way.

For the believer, there is proven eternal hope in Jesus Christ. We know that the hope we have is eternal in nature. Therefore, Peter is encouraging us to focus on something that does not end with this life.

He is telling the Christians that Christ suffered, leaving us an example and that example was to go all the way. When a Christian comes to that place where he or she is willing to go all the way, even if it means to suffer wrongly because of following God, then we identify with Jesus Christ Himself and exemplify the union we have with Him. The union with Christ comes into full view when we suffer wrongly.

Peter goes on to describe the reaction of Jesus as He suffered. God graciously does not leave us with the fact of suffering, but gives an inside look at our example of suffering. Peter quotes Isaiah 53:9, "Who committed no sin, nor was deceit found in His mouth; who, when He was reviled, did not revile in return; when He suffered, He did not threaten, but committed Himself to Him who judges righteously; who Himself bore our sins in His own body on the tree, that we, having died to sins, might live for righteousness."

Jesus suffered even though He had committed no sin. Not only that, but there was no deceit to be found coming out of His mouth. If there is anything that tells me Jesus was perfect and without sin, it is the fact that nothing came out of His mouth that would be sinful.

James writes, "For every kind of beast and bird, of reptile and creature of the sea, is tamed and has been tamed by mankind. But no man can tame the tongue."[37] Yet Jesus would speak nothing sinful and His tongue would be controlled by the holiness that He possessed in being fully God.

When He was reviled, He did not revile back. The word revile means to "heap abuse on someone." Jesus had abuse heaped on Him even though He was innocent. What is amazing is that He did not return the abuse.

Have you ever been verbally attacked by someone? Was your immediate response to attack back in an attempt at self-defense? God taught me a valuable lesson on this point years ago. It has been one of the most important things I have ever learned and it follows the example of Jesus.

When someone confronts me, whether they are correct or wrong, if I will humble myself in the situation, God has something for me to learn. I have found this to be true every time. There have been a few times where someone confronted me in an ungodly way. In those times my sinful flesh wanted to rise up in self-defense and attack back. But that is not the way of Jesus. In those times where I reacted in a godly manner, I humbled myself and became quick to listen and slow to speak. I handled the matter with truth and not with mere emotion. This allowed the Spirit of God to reign in the situation.

When we yield to the Spirit of God in any situation, God is magnified in those moments, and we find ourselves acting as Jesus would. The natural response of humanity will always be self-defense. Self-defense may not always be bad within itself. But when self-defense turns into threats, we often end up returning evil for evil. If anyone had the opportunity and reason to stand up against what was happening, it would have been Jesus. But according to the will of the Father, self-defense was not the supreme purpose for which He came. He came for the salvation of humanity. Humility was His course and that course would lead to exaltation.

So, we find Jesus committing Himself to God who judges righteously. It is here that we find our solace, our peace, and our strength to endure hardships and unjust actions. In the end, we understand that God will judge righteously, and even if we die a martyr's death, we will hear Him say, "Enter in to the joy of the Lord." The Christian can honestly confess, "The Lord knows," no matter the situation or circumstance.

History is filled with those who followed Jesus to the end. You do not have to look far to find men and women who gave everything to follow Jesus. From the first martyr of the church, Stephen, to the present day, there are examples of those who decided to humble themselves in obedience to Jesus.

"So, how far do you go in humility?" The answer to this question is simple. You go all the way. We understand that the cross is not a place of death alone, but the place where "wrong" is eternally confronted. When Jesus said, "It is finished," He did not mean, "Finished for the moment!" And by faith in Him, I have now become a partaker with Him in His work. I can rest in that fact knowing neither death nor life, nor angels nor principalities, nor powers, nor things present nor things to come, nor height nor depth, nor any other created thing, shall be able to separate us from the love of God which is in Christ Jesus our Lord.[38]

Romans 6 teaches that our union with Christ has led to the death of the old man who was sinful, corrupt and base. But it also teaches that my union with Christ has led to life.

With the old sinful man dealt with, the believer is now free to live life in God and unto God. Coming to the place of denying yourself will free you up to take up your cross. The cross you take up is yours, and He carries it with you. You are a partaker of His because of your union with Christ. If Jesus willingly took up His cross, then it only makes sense for Him to say to me, "If you desire to follow me, deny yourself and take up your cross." Jesus calls me to come and identify with Him in sacrifice.

The Beautiful Result

There is no doubt that it is amazing to contemplate what taking up our crosses and following Jesus means to us. However, if we stop there we will not see the amazing masterpiece of God's sovereignty.

Consider that Jesus took up His cross for others. First, it was the will of God, and that will desired salvation for humanity. On the cross, Jesus incurred the full wrath of God because judgment for sin was death. He was sinless and could, therefore, offer the perfect sacrifice of Himself and through His divinity cover the sins of who would by faith turn to Him for salvation. His death dealt specifically with the sins of others. As we contemplated at the beginning of the chapter, this One offered the sacrifice of Himself. But, He took up His cross for others.

When Jesus asks those who would follow Him to deny

themselves and take up their cross, the question is, "For whom are they taking up their cross?" Surely, it is clear that salvation was secured through Jesus Christ, and we who are in union with Him partake in His death and resurrection. So, could it be that when we take up our cross it is for others as well?

Our identification with Christ and taking up our cross becomes an expression of His salvation to the world. As it were, our lives become so empowered by the Spirit of God through our life in Christ that we amplify the work of Jesus Christ for all to see and hear.

We become the mouthpiece of salvation. We are a stroke of color in the masterpiece being painted by the Master's hand. We are the instruments in the hands of the Composer that play the song of salvation to a lost world.

Yes, taking up our cross changes our lives, but just as important, it takes the message of salvation to others. If we will not deny ourselves and take up our cross then we will never live a life of sacrifice that takes the gospel to the ends of the earth. We will miss the blessing of being used by God, trading off the goodness of God for the corrupt desires of unfulfilled humanity. Commit yourself to the Savior, and by His strength deny yourself and then take up your cross. Then you will be able to understand the power of what it means to follow Him.

QUESTIONS FOR REFLECTION:

- What does it look like for you to deny yourself and take up your cross?
- Ask the Lord to search your heart and show you any areas of pride and rebellion. Agree with God and let Him work in your life.
- What would it look like for you to humble yourself before God this day? How might it change your actions, speech, and attitude?

CHALLENGE:

Take time today and consider what to looks like to take up your cross. Write down, in specific terms, what it would look like if you laid down your will and your desires. If you're struggling with this, take it to the Lord and be honest about where you are at this moment and ask Him to help you.

CHAPTER 12

Follow Me

THIS LAST ASPECT OF JESUS' INVITATION IS SO closely aligned with taking up your cross that I only separate it for the purpose of writing and teaching. While I do believe this is a process, I also believe that it can be an instantaneous one. If a believer comes to that place where they, at once, leave it all behind and choose to follow Christ, they have become a true disciple. It may take time to unpack what it means, but the fact is that it does not necessarily take months or years to decide to follow Christ.

Before Paul was ever an apostle he was Saul the Pharisee. He was so convinced that he was doing the work of God that he was willing to stand by and see the followers of Jesus executed. So zealous was this man that he even obtained letters from the high priest to leave the country of Israel and go to Damascus to find these followers of "The Way," as they were called.

On the road to Damascus, the Lord Jesus confronted Saul. This meeting left Saul on the ground and blinded with no option but to listen to the words of Jesus. From that point he was led blind to the city. He sat blind in that city for three days and neither ate nor drank.

I believe Saul sat there remembering all that he had stood for in his supposed service to God. However, in ignorance had missed the central truth of who Jesus really was. All those he had persecuted, all the deaths he had overseen, flooded his mind in those days. I believe the three days of not eating or drinking were a response to the crushing devastation he felt at being found standing against God.

At that point, he was nothing but broken. In those three days he prayed and while he was praying he had a vision that a man named Ananias would lay hands on him and he would receive his sight.

What is interesting about the text is that Ananias is called a disciple. Jesus meets Saul on the road. And Saul has to ask, "Who are you Lord?" Jesus comes to Ananias the disciple and his response is, "Here I am Lord." The contrast of the two statements shows the difference between the heart of a disciple and everyone else. Not only is there a relationship, but also there is a specific availability in the disciple that is found in no other.

Saul was with the disciples at Damascus for a few days. And immediately he proclaimed in the synagogues, saying, "He is the Son of God." The conversion of Saul and his surrender to the will of God was immediate. The man Saul would later be called Paul, the Apostle, and he would go on to spread the message of Jesus into Europe.

The point is that when one has truly trusted in the Lord and been saved, then they are a follower of Christ. The question then becomes, "What kind of follower are they?" Paul's surrender was a matter of fact and for us it will be as well. The point where we come to surrender to the Lordship of Jesus Christ sets us on a path into the will of God.

It is of utmost importance for new believers to be discipled. They need to learn and work through what this salvation means and how it affects their entire life. No one would assume that a baby could grow on his or her own, learn to live and survive without the help of another. In the same fashion, a new believer grows in the context of a family.

While every believer has the indwelling Spirit of God to guide, teach and reveal, God also calls the church to go make disciples. Many of those I have discipled had been Christians for some time. Many of them have said they wished they had someone pouring into their life when they were new believers. The comment usually goes something like this, "I wish I would have had this years ago. Then I would not have made some of the mistakes in my past."

As believers, it is our work to yield to the Spirit of God who is working in our lives and teach others to do the same. If you have come to the place where you have denied yourself and chosen to take up your cross, then I would dare say you are on the path to following Christ. Following Christ is simple, and it can be summed up in three words: trust, yield, and obey.

Trust

That may seem a bit simplistic, but you will find that is the way to a godly life. First you must trust. Trust Jesus as Savior, and trust that He is the God who never leaves nor forsakes. Trust that He is the one who has sent the Holy Spirit into your life to guide, encourage and correct. Trust that He will complete that which He began in you. Never forget that you can trust in His sure return. One day Jesus Christ will return, and He will finish what He has started. Trust this promise.

Yield

Yield to Jesus in submission. He is Lord. Not only is He Lord, but He is the Lord who is loving, gracious, and full of mercy. If Jesus has set his love upon you, then He will love you through all eternity. His love is not conditional. Our actions cannot turn His love from us. And His love for us draws us to Himself. Yielding to the Lord means simply yielding to his unfolding love, grace, and mercy. Yielding to Him is letting go of death and letting life reign.

Obey

Obedience happens once you yield. Yielding means you are willing to receive what is given to you. Obedience is acting on what He has said. Obedience to Jesus will always be in accordance with the will of God as it is expressed in the Bible. Obedience in any situation allows the Holy Spirit to work in that situation. The Spirit is always working to bring the believer into the perfect will of God. Romans 8:26-27 reveals, "The Spirit also helps in our weaknesses. For we do not know what we should pray for as we ought, but the Spirit Himself makes intercession for us with groanings which cannot be uttered. Now He who searches the hearts knows what the mind of the Spirit is, because He makes intercession for the saints according to the will of God."

The Word of God tells us that we do not even know what to pray for so many times, but the Spirit of God intercedes for us. The Spirit of God was sent into our hearts and now takes us with our issues, and takes them to God the Father. C. H. Dodd remarked, "The God in us intercedes to the God above us." How wonderful it is to know that God knows what I need. God knows what is coming, and the Spirit of God is working to prepare us for life and eternity.

Where disobedience quenches the Spirit, our obedience in Jesus quenches the desires of the flesh, allowing us to walk with God. This is the heart of what it is to follow

Jesus. With this being understood, the next question usually is, "How do I know the will of God for a specific situation in life?"

Admittedly, the path before us is often unclear. Which path to choose or decision to make can be difficult at times. Begin with what you know to be the will of God. There are some things that God spells out clearly for humanity. For example, the Word of God says you are to grow in Christ-likeness and mature as a believer. But what about those decisions that are not so clear?

One of my heroes is George Muller. He lived in the late 19th century. He was a man of faith who had come to the Lord as a young man. He would eventually go on to build a large orphanage and a number of schools that changed the lives of thousands of children. Muller gave these orphans a place to grow in love, learn the Word of God, and be trained in a skill that would carry them through life. Over 10,000 orphans were cared for during his ministry. George Muller had walked with God for many years and he had a particular and scriptural way of determining the will of God for a specific situation.

I received a book on George Muller called, *Answers to Prayer* that had been compiled by A.E.C. Brooks. In the beginning of that book Brooks records Muller's way of seeking the will of God.

I seek at the beginning to get my heart into such a state that it has no will of its own in regard to a given matter. Nine-tenths of the difficulties are overcome when our hearts are ready to do the Lord's will, whatever it may be. When one is truly in this state, it is usually but a little way to the knowledge of what His will is.

Having done this, I do not leave the result to feeling or simple impressions. If so, I make myself liable to great delusions.

I seek the will of the Spirit of God through or in connection with the Word of God. The Spirit and the Word must be combined. If I look to the Spirit alone without the Word, I lay myself open to great delusions also.

Next, I take into account providential circumstances. These plainly indicate God's will in connection with His Word and Spirit.

I ask God in prayer to reveal His will to me aright.

Thus through prayer to God, the study of the Word and reflection, I come to a deliberate judgment according to the best of my ability and knowledge, and if my mind is thus at peace, and continues so after two or three more petitions, I proceed accordingly. In trivial matters and transactions involving most important issues, I have found this method always effective.

There is great wisdom in Muller's words. The will of God is found deliberately and not by chance. That is not to say there will be times when the way seems unclear, but in the end as you walk by faith, you begin to recognize God's leading. When there is a heart of yielded obedience, the will of God will not be far away.

With that being said, the Christian must also never forget that walking in faith is essential to living out the will of God. There comes a point for trusting God and stepping out in faith. When we live by faith, and that faith leads us to obedience, then we begin to experience the joy of being in the will of God. This is what it means to follow Christ.

QUESTIONS FOR REFLECTION:

- What has God been doing in your heart over these past days?
- How well do you believe you follow Christ?
- Are you yielding to His work and direction in your life?
- Is your life characterized by obedience?
- What areas of your life do you need wisdom and direction?

CHALLENGE:

Take George Muller's concept of seeking God to find His will and begin to use it in your life. Is there a decision that you need to make? Seek the Lord and His wisdom, trusting that He will guide you into His will.

CHAPTER 13

Sacrifice and Blessing

I appeal to you therefore, brothers by the mercies of God, that you present your bodies a living sacrifice, holy, acceptable to God, which is your reasonable service. And do not be conformed to this world, but be transformed by the renewing of your mind, that you may prove what is that good and acceptable and perfect will of God.

Romans 12:1, 2

PAUL COMES TO THIS PLACE IN HIS LETTER TO the Romans, having laid the strong foundation for man's rejection of God and the deserved judgment. He then goes on to give the answer to God's judgment—that is God's salvation through faith in Jesus Christ. Now in salvation, we have been freed from the penalty of sin and freed from the law to live in the grace of God.

He then goes on to explain Israel's rejection of the Messiah—that the Gentiles might hear the gospel and that in the end, Israel would not totally reject her Messiah. He ends chapter 11 in awestruck wonder with these words,

"For who has known the mind of the Lord? Or who has become His counselor?" "Or who has first given to Him and it shall be repaid to him?" For of Him and through Him and to Him are all things, to whom be glory forever. Amen."

It is as if Paul loses himself in the wonderful truth of God and what flows from his heart is no less than three different passages from the Old Testament.[39] Paul then switches from theological teaching to this intense application of the truth he has just spoken by appealing hearers and readers, based on all that he had written in explaining the mercy of God. His appeal is to present your bodies a living sacrifice, holy and acceptable to God, which is your reasonable service.

To present our bodies as a living sacrifice reminds us of Old Testament sacrifice in which the animal is laid upon the altar and sacrificed. The difference here seems to be that the Old Testament offering died. Now we are living sacrifices. What looks to be a paradox is actually a description of how to live the Christian life.

Jesus has already paid the perfect sacrifice. He has completed the task. The believer now has at once been given life and freedom to live for the glory of God as one who has been set free. Paul urges the believer to offer up his or her life as a living sacrifice. And our sacrifice has been made holy and acceptable to God through the work of Jesus Christ.

Therefore, it is only logical that we present ourselves to God with a heart of worship. He has given us life. He has made us holy, and now we come to Him in an act of worship. All that we have to offer is the life that He has given us.

It is important to note that the sacrifice of our lives does not secure salvation because that was the work of Jesus Christ. Rather, we offer our lives back to God so that He might be magnified through our lives. Jesus calls us to take up our crosses and follow Him. If we do not come to a place of surrender and sacrifice, it is doubtful that we will ever enter into obedience and live the powerfully joyous life of making disciples.

Jesus showed us what it was to live this life by presenting Himself continually to God. His life is our example. His spirit is our power. His Word is our guide. Let us continually follow the Savior and present our lives to Him in worship.

Paul then goes on to say, "And do not be conformed to this world, but be transformed by the renewing of your mind." The idea of being "conformed" is one of being outwardly molded by some force. For the Christian, we are not to be molded outwardly by the forces of this world. Much of the Western church has allowed itself to be molded into a worldly image. When this happens, we lose our distinctiveness and the ability to speak truth. The Christian, who is molded to look like this world is the ultimate hypocrite. As a Christian, the Spirit of God continually seeks to remind and convict the believer that they are to look like Jesus and not like this world. There is only one way to combat this worldly force and that is inward transformation.

That life transformation begins by having your mind renewed by the Spirit of God. The world tries to press the believer into its mold while the Holy Spirit seeks to transform the believer inwardly. What happens in the mind and heart of humanity is eventually displayed in the actions.

Jesus said, "What comes out of a man, that defiles a man. For from within, out of the heart of men, proceed evil thoughts, adulteries, fornications, murders, thefts, covetousness, wickedness, deceit, lewdness, an evil eye, blasphemy, pride, foolishness."[40]

The heart gives directions for actions and the actions lead to a way of life. When God changes and renews the heart of someone, then the life of that person will give evidence of that inward change.

Paul then concludes this phrase by saying that when your mind is renewed, you will know that good and acceptable and perfect will of God. Unless we are lost or in rebellion, we want to know what is the His will.

Jesus presented Himself to the Father in the Garden of Gethsemane. There He chose the will of God for His life by accepting the fact that the Father's will was for Him to go to the cross. He denied Himself.

This led Jesus to go to the cross and present Himself as a sacrifice for the sins of humanity. Because Jesus was willing to humble Himself and become obedient to death, even death on the cross, The Father therefore exalted Him and gave Him the name that is above every name. All will bow and confess before Him. His humiliation preceded his exaltation, and it will be the same with us. Jesus calls the believer. Deny yourself, take up your cross, and follow Him. Will you be a disciple so that you may then go and make one?

Concluding Remarks

In life we often hear of "what we need to be doing." But just as important as "what" is the question of "how?" Following God and making disciples is about accomplishing the will of God in the power of God under the direction of God. The way down that path is found in Scripture.While the main purpose of this book is to help you personally understand what it means to be a disciple, the result should end up with you making disciples. There is no need to overthink what this might look like, but I find some suggestions are always helpful.

First, be a disciple. The integrity of the Christian life only comes through walking with Jesus. It is not learned behavior but a transformed heart. When you teach others the idea of "Nevertheless" you will be reminded as well. Work through what this looks like in your life, understanding that your experience, your struggle, and your victory exist for a reason.

Second, seek to leave people better than when you found them. If they do not know Jesus, tell them about Him. If they need help, help them. If encouragement is needed, give it. If you will live this way, there will be no lack of people into which you can pour your life. One of the greatest agents of change I have ever seen is a 5-foot tall young woman who has the heart of Jesus. She is always looking to encourage others, and God brings people to her all the time. She shares Jesus, walks with them through difficulty, and loves them. You might never know her name, but God does and He uses her often. I cannot tell you the number of people that have been changed because she took time to care.

Third, be intentional. Look for opportunities where you can walk with people through a season of life. The whole point of *Go Disciple* is to walk with others. As you walk with them, you show and teach them what it means to follow Jesus. Do not worry about being perfect or saying the right thing all the time. Be available, pray, and go for it. The only way to be a disciple who makes disciples is to get out there and do it. No amount of training can take the place of doing.

Fourth, disciple to make disciples. Always go into discipleship with the idea of making a disciple who understands the end goal is for them to go and do the same with others. There is a lot of teaching in the world that ends with depositing knowledge. This should never be the goal, and it will not be for the one who understands the Spirit's work of salvation and sanctification in the expanding Kingdom of God.

Fifth, walk by faith. Trust that God makes up the difference in our shortcomings as we seek to be a disciple and make disciples. Replace fear with faith and then go do it. Leave the results up to God. He will not let you down. He is your help.

May God bless your journey. Go disciple.

QUESTIONS FOR REFLECTION:

- Will you commit to being a disciple of Jesus Christ?
- Being a disciple inherently includes making disciples. How will you allow God to help you grow and go make disciples?

CHALLENGE:

Have you come to the place where you can honestly say, "Not my will, but your will be done?" Spend time with the Lord, asking Him to search your heart for the answer. Whatever He brings to your attention, agree with Him.

Endnotes

1   I Corinthians 13:11
2   I John 1:3
3   Philippians 2:1
4   Luke 10:27
5   Ephesians 1:13, 14
6   I Thessalonians 2:13
7   Philippians 2:13
8   http://www.reformed.org/documents/WSC.html question 87
9   Romans 7:18
10   http://1828.mshaffer.com/d/search/word,awful - find book format
11   http://www.merriam-webster.com/dictionary/follower?show=0&t=1296132488
12   New Linguistic and Exegetical Key to the Greek New Testament by Cleon L. Rogers Jr.
        and Cleon L. Rogers III (Oct 1, 1998)
13   I John 3:15
14   2 Corinthian 6:14, 15
15   Philippians 3:8
16   Genesis 3:8, 9
17   2 Corinthians 5:21
18   Philippians 2:13
19   I Corinthians 2:13
20   Revelation 4:9-11
21   Isaiah 6:5 NKJV
22   Ephesians 5:15 HCSB
23   I John 2:6
24   Matthew 5:14 HCSB
25   John 1:4,5
26   Ephesians 2:19
27   1 Corinthians 9:24-27
28   Matthew 26:36ff
29   Exodus 27:20
30   The Greek word is plen, which can be translated by the words nevertheless,
        notwithstanding, but rather, etc. "Nevertheless" is the translation in the New King
        James Bible
31   Hebrews 9:26
32   Hebrews 10:11
33   Galatians 2:20
34   John 4:24
35   Luke 10:27
36   John 14:21
37   James 3:7, The First 11 verses are a discussion on the tongue and fact that what we
        speak reveals the state the heart.
38   Romans 8:38, 39 NKJV
39   Scriptures included by Paul Isaiah 40:13 Who has directed the Spirit of the Lord, Or as
        His counselor has taught Him? , Jeremiah 23:18 For who has stood in the counsel of
        the Lord, And has perceived and heard His word? Who has marked His word and heard
        it?, Job 41:11 Who has preceded Me, that I should pay him? Everything under heaven is
        Mine.
40   Mark 7:20-22 NKJV

41296662R00083

Made in the USA
Middletown, DE
08 March 2017